The DIY Wedding Manual

Visit our How To website at www.howto.co.uk

At **www.howto.co.uk** you can engage in conversation with our authors – all of whom have 'been there and done that' in their specialist fields. You can get access to special offers and additional content but most importantly you will be able to engage with, and become a part of, a wide and growing community of people just like yourself.

At **www.howto.co.uk** you'll be able to talk and share tips with people who have similar interests and are facing similar challenges in their lives. People who, just like you, have the desire to change their lives for the better - be it through moving to a new country, starting a new business, growing their own vegetables, or writing a novel.

At **www.howto.co.uk** you'll find the support and encouragement you need to help make your aspirations a reality.

You can go direct to **www.the-diy-wedding-guide.co.uk** which is part of the main How To site.

How To Books strives to present authentic, inspiring, practical information in their books. Now, when you buy a title from **How To Books**, you get even more than just words on a page.

The DIY Wedding Manual

How to create your perfect day
without a celebrity budget

Lisa Sodeau

howtobooks

Published by How To Books Ltd
Spring Hill House, Spring Hill Road
Begbroke, Oxford OX5 1RX
Tel: (01865) 375794. Fax: (01865) 379162
info@howtobooks.co.uk
www.howtobooks.co.uk

How To Books greatly reduce the carbon footprint of their books by
sourcing their typesetting and printing in the UK.

First published 2010
Reprinted 2011

British Library Cataloguing in Publication Data
A catalogue record for this book is available from the British Library

ISBN: 978 1 84528 405 3

Illustrations by James Sodeau
Produced for How To Books by Deer Park Productions, Tavistock
Typeset by Pantek Arts Ltd, Maidstone, Kent
Printed and bound by Bell & Bain Ltd, Glasgow

☙ Contents ☙

Contents

Preface

Congratulations you're engaged – this is where the real fun begins! Over the next few months you'll have lots of decisions to make as you plan your dream day. You may already have in mind exactly what you want from your special day, or you may not. Don't worry, this book is bursting with ideas and, best of all, it's for brides with realistic budgets.

As you progress with your wedding plans you'll start to realise how expensive weddings can be, but with a little help and guidance from this book you'll have the wedding day of your dreams without starting married life in debt!

So sit back, unhook the phone, grab a notepad to jot down any ideas and enjoy your time as a bride-to-be – you're going to make it the best day of your life!

Wedding timeline

Organising a wedding can seem like a huge, daunting task and it may make you feel stressed rather than elated that you're a bride-to-be. With so much to organise, how do you fit it all into your everyday life? The secret is to tackle each area one step at a time rather than attempt to do everything at once. Take a look at the simple breakdown below to guide you through the different areas and help you work out an order to tackle them in.

- ❀ Decide on a date
- ❀ Set a budget
- ❀ Decide on the number of guests and make a list
- ❀ Send out save the date cards if needed
- ❀ Research and visit possible venues
- ❀ Book a ceremony and reception venue
- ❀ Look into wedding insurance and decide on the best policy for you
- ❀ Research and book the photographer
- ❀ Choose the best man, ushers, bridesmaids, pageboys and flower girls
- ❀ Start wedding dress and shoe shopping
- ❀ Start looking for the bridesmaids' dresses and shoes
- ❀ Start looking for the grooms' and ushers' suits
- ❀ Research and book caterers and marquees if needed
- ❀ Choose and book wedding cars
- ❀ Book entertainment for the reception
- ❀ Start getting paperwork in order
- ❀ Send invitations out five to six months in advance with your gift list information
- ❀ Decide on your wedding flowers
- ❀ Order your wedding rings
- ❀ Book the toastmaster if you're having one

❀ Let your venue and caterers know the exact numbers of guests and any special dietary information

❀ Start your wedding hair and makeup trials

❀ Book your honeymoon

❀ Book your wedding night accommodation

❀ Decide on the table plan for the wedding breakfast and give a copy to your venue

❀ Order your wedding cake

❀ Arrange your favours if you're having them

❀ Start designing and making the table plan, place names and order of service books

❀ Get married!

❀ Go on honeymoon

❀ Order the professional wedding photographs

❀ Send out thank you cards

❀ Relax…

⇒ *Stationery* ⇐

Many couples use their wedding stationery to set the style and colour theme for their whole day. With save the date cards, day and evening invites, RSVP cards, place cards and thank you cards all required, designing and making your own stationery can save you a fortune! From simple designs to more unique ideas, your stationery is a reflection of your wedding day dream, so make it a special keepsake you'll cherish for many years to come.

SETTING A COLOUR PALETTE

Deciding on a colour palette for your wedding is an important decision. It will help set the style and theme for the whole day, as well as help to set up guidelines for choosing other elements such as flowers, bridesmaid dresses, the wedding cake, the wedding stationery, and perhaps it will even inspire the mother of the bride's outfit. Having a colour palette to refer to will help ensure your day doesn't turn into a multi-coloured rainbow!

The first time you will need to use your colour palette will be when you send out your save the date cards, or invitations if you're not sending out save the date cards. It's a good idea to decide on your colour palette as early as possible so you don't end up panicking and choosing just any colours at the last minute. It's really important to choose your colour palette and theme (if you're having one) before designing the stationery and not the other way round.

How to decide on a colour palette

At first, choosing a colour palette may seem like a huge task and you may not know where to start. Don't panic. Try to answer these questions to give you a clearer indication of what you like:

- Do you have a favourite colour(s)?
- Which season are you getting married in? You should use warm colours like browns and reds in the winter months to create a cosy ambience, and avoid using dark colours during a summer wedding unless they're contrasted with light colours, like black and light blue.
- If you have already selected a venue, what type of ambience does it create? Is it old and traditional or modern and funky?
- Do you have a particular theme or era in mind for your wedding day? Perhaps you would like to wear a vintage dress or set a theme like a garden party?
- Do you have a favourite flower you are planning on using in your wedding bouquet? Which colours does the flower come in?

Answering these questions should help to set some foundations for your colour palette. You can have as little as two colours in your palette but try to avoid using more than four, as this will over-complicate the colour scheme and make it look messy. Choose one or two colours as the main colour and use any others as accents (where they will only be used in small amounts). Think about using tones or hues in your colour scheme too.

Example colour schemes

Here are some sample colour palettes to inspire your colour scheme. Try using one as a base and adapt it for your own wedding.

Traditional
- Cream and pink
- Lavender and light blue
- White and cream
- Gold and silver
- Lavender and ivory

❀ Ivory and mint green
❀ Grey and pale pink

Modern

❀ Black and pale pink
❀ Black and white
❀ Chocolate brown and blue
❀ Chocolate brown and pink
❀ Aqua blue and black
❀ Red and pink
❀ Black and teal

SETTING A WEDDING THEME

When you set your colour scheme you will probably have an idea of the type of theme you want to carry through your day. For many, the theme will be a traditional white wedding with accents of pastel colours for summer weddings or deeper shades for winter weddings. However, you can choose a theme for your wedding based on your personalities or interests you both share to make your day more memorable.

Here is a selection of wedding theme suggestions for your special day, ranging from traditional to something more unique.

Seasonal wedding

❀ Spring – Hold your wedding in spring to signify a new beginning. A spring wedding can be full of pastel shades such as yellow and vibrant greens. Images of butterflies, birds, rabbits and flowers can all be included as part of your wedding day theme. Choose traditional spring flowers for your day such as daffodils and tulips.
❀ Summer – A glorious and hopefully sunny time to get married. From pale pinks to vibrant purples, most colours suit a summer wedding. Choose refreshing fruit punches and BBQ food for the wedding breakfast to reflect the season.

❀ Autumn – With the world turning into hues of orange, red and brown around you, an autumn wedding can be a vibrant affair! Choose bouquets of burnt orange and red flowers with twisted willow and dark red berries and leaves. Groomsmen can wear orange or red ties and waistcoats to match the bridesmaids' dresses.

❀ Winter – Create a magical winter wonderland. Use lots of silver and white throughout the day and decorate your tables and topiary in fairy lights and glitter for a sparkly ambience. Hire a smoke machine for that extra 'wow' factor!

Easter

Use shades of baby yellow, blue and green for the colour theme. Think about representing the time of year by giving out small chocolate eggs as the favours and painting the place names onto hard-boiled eggs placed on a nest of feathers and ribbon.

Valentines

Think pink and red. Use lots of hearts throughout the day, starting with the stationery through to heart-shaped favours and wedding fairy cakes. Roses in red, white and pink are a perfect flower choice for this type of wedding.

Oriental

Use hues of black, white and red to reflect an oriental theme. Choose simple flowers such as oriental lilies and decorate your venue with white candles for a clean crisp look. For an interesting twist, swap your cutlery for chopsticks and use square plates instead of circular ones. Give out fortune cookies as your wedding favours.

A one-colour theme

Take your favourite colour and use it in different shades as the theme for your wedding day. For example, if your favourite colour is pink, decorate your venue with pink balloons, have a jar of pink marshmellows on the wedding tables, a tower of pink cupcakes for the wedding cake and lots of pink flowers!

Hollywood glamour

Think of your favourite film star or stars and create your whole day around them. Have a black tie dress code and serve cocktails in posh martini glasses. You can play music from your actor's era and even hire look-alikes to mingle with your guests for an extra surprise!

Beach theme

Why travel abroad to go to the beach when you can create your own at home! Have a relaxed dress code and serve your guests drinks like Caribbean punch and pina coladas. You can decorate your venue with palm trees and shells and even have areas of sand for the children to play in.

DECIDING ON FONTS

After setting your colour palette, you will have a clearer idea of whether you want your wedding day to have a traditional or modern theme and this will be reflected in the fonts you use on your stationery.

For a traditional feel use script and italic fonts such as:

- Century Schoolbook Italic
- Edwardian Script
- Electra Italic
- Fette Fraktur
- Garamond Italic
- Goudy Old Style
- ITC Bookman Italic
- ITC Galliard
- Medici Script
- Old English Text

1 (a)

Miss Natalie Davis
and Mr. Kieran Fox

request the honour of your presence
at their marriage

on the 21st September 2011
at the Queens Summer Club, Cambridge

Formal invite to follow

(b)

Miss Natalie Davis
and Mr. Kieran Fox

request the honour of your presence
at their marriage

on the 21st September 2011
at the Queens Summer Club, Cambridge

Formal invite to follow

2 (a)

Miss Natalie Davis
and Mr. Kieran Fox

request the honour of your presence
at their marriage

on the 21st September 2011
at the Queens Summer Club, Cambridge

Formal invite to follow

(b)

Miss Natalie Davis
and Mr. Kieran Fox

request the honour of your presence
at their marriage

on the 21st September 2011
at the Queens Summer Club, Cambridge

Formal invite to follow

3 (a)

Miss Natalie Davis
and Mr. Kieran Fox

request the honour of your presence
at their marriage

on the 21st September 2011
at the Queens Summer Club,
Cambridge

Formal invite to follow

(b)

Miss Natalie Davis
and Mr. Kieran Fox

request the honour of your
presence at their marriage

on the twenty first of September,
two thousand and eleven,
at the Queens Summer
Club, Cambridge

Formal invite to follow

1(a) Save the date card using Edwardian Script, **(b)** Save the date card using Edwardian Script and ITC Galliard Bold

2(a) Save the date card using Medici Script Medium, **(b)** Save the date card using Times Italic and ITC Galliard Italic

3(a) Save the date card using AvantGarde Medium, **(b)** Save the date card using Helvetica Neue 45 Light and AvantGarde Medium

❀ Snell Rounded
❀ Times

For a modern feel use sans-serif fonts. These are fonts without ascenders and descenders so the font appears much rounder, shorter and cleaner. Try these fonts for a modern look:

❀ Arial
❀ Avant Garde
❀ Bauhaus
❀ Century Gothic
❀ Comic Sans

❁ Helvetica
❁ Marker Felt

A popular way to lay out a modern-looking invite is to start with large text that gradually gets smaller or to spell out numbers, for example 'on the sixth of June, two thousand and eleven'. You can also use different weights or colours to highlight important words, for example place the bride's and groom's names in bold or the date and time in italics.

SAVE THE DATE CARDS

As a general rule, you send out your wedding invites five to six months in advance. However if you're getting married abroad or in a busy season like the summer months or around a special celebration such as Christmas or Valentine's day, or if you are simply worried that important people to you may not be able to make it without receiving more notice, sending out save the date cards can be a very good idea. You can send them out as soon as you've set a date, even if you haven't booked a venue. But you should avoid sending them out much over a year in advance in case the card gets lost or forgotten about!

Save the date cards can contain as much or as little information as you want. Apart from the date, you can include the venue location if you already know it or you may want to save this information for your invites. If you are getting married abroad, you'll probably want to send out your invites earlier than the usual five to six months in advance to allow your guests to plan their time off work and save up money to pay for the trip. In this case it would be a good idea to put the location on the save the date cards to get the ball rolling, followed shortly by the invites when you have booked your venue.

Wording examples

Here are some examples of save the date wording for you to adapt to suit your wedding style.

Casual

Charlotte Wood and James Green
are getting married!
Please save the 16th June 2011 to attend our special day
Invites to follow

A date to remember!
27th June 2011
Please save the date to attend the wedding of
Claire and Phillip
at Chislehurst cricket ground
Formal invite to follow

Formal wording

Miss Natalie Davis
and Mr Kieran Fox
request the honour of your presence
at their marriage
on the 21st September 2011
at the Queens' Summer Club, Cambridge
Formal invite to follow

Mr and Mrs Edward Smythe
request the honour of your presence
at the marriage of their daughter
Elizabeth Rose
to
Mr James Anthony
on 10th July 2011
Formal invite to follow

Designing a save the date card

Save the date cards should be simple and inexpensive to produce. You want
to save the 'wow' factor for your invitations, so these cards should look
relatively simple. The cheapest way to send a save the date card is to send

out an email. While this can be the easiest way to tell people, remember that not everyone may have access to email, and the colours and fonts you can use may be limited.

A prettier alternative to a straightforward email is to email round a PDF of your save the date card. This means that you can design your card using any font or colour and any size or shape. It can then be emailed as an attachment for your guests to print out and keep. Any relatives or friends without access to email can be given a print out of the card. This method is by far the cheapest and, best of all, it's environmentally friendly!

A save the date card doesn't technically have to be a card. There are lots of fun and unique ways of giving your guests the information they need. The most obvious way is to send out a small card in your chosen wedding colours with some reference to your wedding theme if you have one. Here are some ideas to get you started.

Easy card idea

Two pieces of card mounted onto each other. For example, if your theme is black and white you can mount a piece of white card on a piece of black card. You can finish this off by decorating with some black or white beads, hearts, stickers or a ribbon that ties round the card.

Shaped cards

If you would like to send a card but think that this may be a little boring, cut your card into a shape to match your theme. Always make a template of your chosen shape to make it easier for you to make each one exactly the same. Just remember to make sure your chosen shape fits into an envelope!

Fridge magnets

There are lots of companies advertised on the internet who can produce fridge magnets as save the date cards. They have the information on the front and the magnet stuck to the back. Some designs even have enough room for a small photograph to be printed on them too. They make a very useful and cherished keepsake!

Chocolates

Why not send a chocolate with your save the date cards – your guests will be sure to remember your wedding date!

Postcard

If you're getting married abroad, then a postcard makes the perfect save the date card. You can have a photograph of the two of you on the front and all the details of the wedding on the back. Saving on envelope costs is an advantage of this type of save the date card.

Packet of flower seeds

For a unique and romantic idea, send your guests a homemade pack of seeds for them to plant. The seeds could be a flower from your wedding bouquet or just your favourite flower. All the information for your wedding can be printed on the outside of the packet. Your guests will love the idea of a flower blooming as your wedding day approaches.

Box of confetti

This is similar to the seeds idea, but your guests will be able to bring along the confetti to throw on your wedding day. Be sure to check with your venue that they allow confetti to be thrown. You can consider making your own biodegradable confetti by drying out some flower petals and, like the flower seeds packet, all the information can be printed on the outside of the box. The idea of confetti will be sure to get across the hint that a wedding is happening soon!

When designing your save the date cards, you should keep in mind how they will work alongside your invitations as a set. Your invitations should be an extension of the save the date card and your other stationery such as place cards and thank-you cards. Each element of your wedding stationery should carry through your wedding day theme and style.

INVITATIONS

Ideally you should aim to send out your invitations five to six months before your wedding. Your invitation should contain all the information your guests need to know including:

- ❀ Who is hosting the wedding
- ❀ Date and time
- ❀ Ceremony and reception venue
- ❀ How and by when to RSVP
- ❀ Any other special information such as directions, hotels in the area, any special dietary requests, if children are not welcome

Wording examples

Here are some examples of invitation wording for you to adapt to suit your wedding style.

Casual

Claire Taylor and David Lindman
would like to invite you to help celebrate their wedding
on 21st March 2011
at All Saints Church, Westminster, London
at 3 o'clock
followed by a reception at the Swan and Mitre Inn, Westminster, London
Please RSVP with any special dietary requests by 15th January 2011

Formal

The honour of your presence is requested at the marriage of
Miss Anna Beth Wright
to
Mr Francis Stevens
on Saturday the First of June
Two Thousand and Eleven

at Four o'clock
Syon Park, Middlesex
Followed by an evening reception
RSVP

Contemporary

Together with their families,
Rose Fletcher and Tom Martin
Invite you to share their joy as they are wed
on 13th September Two Thousand and Eleven
Bury Town Hall, Suffolk
at 3 o'clock
Followed by a reception at the nearby Buckley Manor
RSVP

Designing an invitation

It is easy to make beautiful handmade invites without needing to be a craft expert. Handmade invites are lovely to receive and your guests will appreciate the time and effort you have put into them. What puts most people off making their own cards is that they think that they are too complicated to make, but you can make them as simple or as extravagant as you like. And if you think you won't have enough time to make invites for everyone, just make them for the most important people to you who will cherish them the most and give everyone else pre-bought cards instead.

How to make an invitation

There are many different styles of invites for you to consider – from simple folded cards to more complicated folding techniques, there's an invite suitable for every bride!

Firstly, you need to decide on a style to match your wedding colour scheme and theme. Next you need to buy enough card for the invite you want to send. Remember you will need to buy envelopes to fit your invites, so think about that before creating any unusual or oversized cards. Remember the thicker the card you choose for your invites, the dearer the postage costs could be for sending them. Here are a few ideas to get your creative juices flowing.

A simple folded card

The easiest cards to make are simply folded. Fold a piece of your chosen sized card in half and insert your written invite inside. The written part of your invite can be either a piece of thin card stuck down on the inside right-hand side of the invite, or it can be a separate folded piece of paper attached through the middle with the staples hidden by a piece of ribbon kept in place along the fold.

To make this simple invite look more stylish, decorate the front. For a more bespoke look, carefully cut out a shape on the front of your invite using a craft knife. You will then be able to see the colour of the folded piece of paper inside. This design may need some practising to get perfect, so practise on some cheap card or paper before attempting it on your final invites.

Pocket and folding invitation

To make something a little more interesting, present your invite in a pocket cardboard envelope or make the invitation so that it is opened either horizontally or vertically. Both of these ideas are great for weddings where you want to enclose several pieces of information such as a RSVP card, map or a wedding gift list.

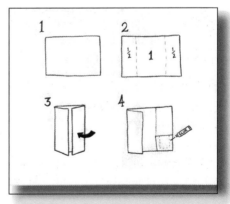

Step-by-step guide to making a pocket and folding invitation

To make a horizontal-folding invitation, take a large piece of card and divide it into three sections. The middle section will be the largest and the left and right sections will each be equal to half the size of the middle section. This means that when you fold the left and right sections into the centre they together make up the size of the middle section and cover it. The middle section will be where you include all your wedding information and your two smaller sections become the opening flaps.

If you want to make a special area for inserting other information, such as a RSVP card, then the inside flaps are an ideal place to do this. Stick a piece of card on the inside of the flaps to make a pocket. This piece of card should be the same width as the width of one of the flaps and should measure a third in height. Stick this piece of card down on the bottom, left and right-hand sides, leaving the top side open, so you can insert other pieces of information into it.

You can tie the invite together with a piece of pretty ribbon or hold it together with a sticker or wax stamp of your initials!

Flower invitation

A flower invite is a more interesting version of the horizontal folding invite, where all four sides fold into the centre and make a flower shape when unfolded.

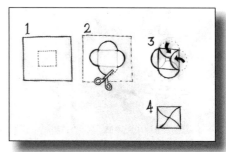

Step-by-step guide to making a flower invitation

Using a large square piece of card, measure and draw up a square centre, leaving room on all four sides around the square shape. Then cut each side into a semi-circle to make the folding flaps, still leaving the centre of the card as a square shape. This will make a shape like a flower with a square centre. Next score the square shape, so each flap can eventually be folded easily into the centre. These flaps will make the outside of the card.

Next stick your wedding information in the centre of your invite, on the square shape. You can decorate the centre with glued-on diamantes, feathers or enclose some dried petals.

Lastly, complete your invitations by folding each flap into the centre in a clockwise direction and close with a sticker, wax seal or ribbon. To send the invites, either insert them into envelopes or use the square back for the address and stamp, saving money on envelope costs.

Decorating your invites

❀ Ribbon – Add a piece of ribbon horizontally across the front and back of your folded invite.

❀ Feathers – Feathers add an expensive and luxurious feel to a wedding theme without actually being expensive. Add a couple to the front of your invite, or enclose a few loose ones inside your card for a lovely surprise when it's opened.

❀ Dried flowers – Perhaps you have a garden party theme or you just want a natural looking invite. Try adding a dried flower to the front of your invite. You can frame it onto another piece of handmade card or paper first and rip the sides instead of cutting, to make it look more natural.

❀ Petals – Enclose a few dried petals or even some confetti in the inside of your invite so your guests get a nice surprise when they open it. This is cheap and cheerful.

❀ Diamantes – For a bling-bling invite, add some diamantes. You can buy these at most craft stores and for easier application buy ones with self-adhesive backs.

❀ Pearl shapes – If you want your invite to have more of a wedding feeling, then a pearl accessory is a must! You can make your own pearl shape such as a heart or circle by using some thin wire bent into your chosen shape and then threaded with small pearl beads. Attach the pearl shape to the front of your card with either super glue or thin wire inserted through the front of the card, with the back covered in a pretty fabric to hide the wire. You can buy pearl beads in most craft or wedding shops.

EVENING INVITES

Of course if money were no object then you would invite everybody you know to your wedding. Unfortunately though, weddings are expensive and as a result you will probably be limited to only inviting a certain number of people to the day part of your wedding. However you will be able to invite the remaining people to the evening reception. Don't be embarrassed to do this and feel obliged to invite everyone to the day part, as your guests will understand how expensive weddings are.

You will need a separate invitation for the evening only guests as it will contain less information than the invitations for the day guests. The evening only invitations should include the following:

- ❀ Date of wedding reception
- ❀ Reception venue
- ❀ Time
- ❀ Whether food will be served
- ❀ How to RSVP
- ❀ Any special information, for example whether children are welcome, special parking instructions, directions and local hotels

Wording examples

Follow one of these wording examples for your evening reception invites:

Casual

Please help us celebrate our wedding
at our evening reception
on Saturday Third April, Two Thousand and Eleven
at Mansfield Gardens, Essex
from 7 o'clock
A finger buffet will be provided

Formal

Mr and Mrs David Williams
Request the pleasure of your company
at the wedding reception for their daughter Sarah Thomas
and
Mr Carl Medway
Friday, Twelfth, December
Two Thousand and Eleven

at Six o'clock
Green Acres Hall, Brentwood, Essex

Designing your evening invites

Try to keep your evening reception invitations looking as close as possible to your save the date cards and day invites so that they all look like a set. The evening invites can be a much smaller size as they will include less information, but you should try and keep the colours, fonts and any finishing touches such as ribbon or jewels looking similar. Use some of the invitation design ideas on page 12 for your evening invites and adapt them to suit your needs.

ORDER OF SERVICE BOOKLET

The order of service is a booklet which contains the complete text of a couple's wedding ceremony and chosen hymns. They are given out to the guests on arrival at the ceremony venue. They are not compulsory to have at your wedding but make a lovely keepsake for you and your family to cherish.

If you want to have order of service booklets at your wedding talk to your ceremony venue about supplying them, or if your venue will charge you for them think about designing and making your own.

TABLE STATIONERY

The next stationery you will be thinking about will be the table stationery such as the menus, place cards, a table plan and table numbers or names. Some venues will supply this stationery as part of their fee, while others may charge extra. If your venue informs you that there will be a charge, you may be tempted to make your own as they are fairly easy to make – all you need is some card, paper, use of a computer or a pen if you have neat handwriting.

How to Organise a Table Plan

Every wedding breakfast must have a table plan. It will be placed in the entrance to the wedding breakfast and your guests will use it to find out where they are sitting. If you don't have one, there will be a lot of confusion and indecision over where to sit (something you don't want to be dealing with on your wedding day) so make sure your venue supplies this or supply your own.

To work out your table plan, first decide on the table shape. Some venues will give you the option of a 'L' shape, horseshoe shape or one long table, while others will offer round or square tables. Next, find out from your venue how many people will comfortably fit round each table – this will give you a clear indication of how many tables you will need and enable you to do the plan.

The easiest way of working out a table plan is to write all the guests' names on separate pieces of paper to enable you to move them round as you plan the tables. Remember to keep in mind the specific needs of your guests, for example you may want to seat elderly guests away from loud speakers and seat guests with children near the toilets.

Here are a few things to take into consideration when doing the table plan:

❀ On rectangular tables partners are usually seated opposite each other, while on round tables they are seated next to one another.
❀ Do you want to sit the guests in alternative sexes?
❀ Small children should always be seated with their parents.
❀ If you are having a separate children's table, only seat children here between the ages of 7 and 12. Teenagers should sit among the other guests.

Once you have your table plan organised and you've decided on your table names, the next thing to do is to make the cards for the centre of the table to co-ordinate with the table plan. Your venue should provide you with the cardholder for the centrepiece, otherwise you can try pinning it to the flower centrepiece or hiring one. See the section on 'Arranging the seating plan' in Chapter 3 for ideas for naming the tables.

If you're using numbers or even a straightforward table name, it is simply a case of printing out (or writing) a number or name on a piece of A5 card and decorating it with your themed items such as ribbon, flowers, etc. If you are using something more unique such as a photograph, it's a good idea to scan and print it onto paper rather than using the original in case it gets lost or forgotten at the end of the day.

PLACE CARDS

Place cards are displayed on the tables to indicate where each guest is sitting. They don't have to be anything complicated – just a folded piece of card displaying the guest's name, decorated with any finishing touches to go with your theme.

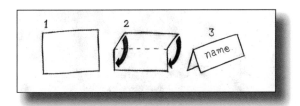

Step-by-step guide to making place cards

Real bride's tip

'Instead of a straightforward written table plan and place cards, we used photographs of the guests. It was really funny and created a great buzz before the guests sat down for dinner.'

THANK YOU CARDS

While you're planning your wedding your thank you cards may seem like a long way off, but it's good to plan what they will look like in advance. As they will be the last contact you have with your wedding guests, make them something they can cherish forever. Try using one of your professional photographs as the image on the thank you cards, as your guests wouldn't have seen these yet, or use a photograph from your honeymoon. Your guests can then frame this image as a cherished keepsake.

Budget busters

Reduce your stationery costs by using some of these great tips:

❀ An alternative to buying a guest book is to make your own. Simply buy a cheap plain notebook and decorate the cover with some pretty fabric and decorations to match your wedding theme and colour scheme.

❀ Another idea for a homemade guest book is to ask the guests to pin cards with their best wishes on to a board or even something prettier like hanging them on a topiary tree.

❀ Double up the use of the favours by having them as place cards too. For example, you could have biscuits or chocolates decorated with the guest's name, serving as both the place card and the favour.

❀ If you're considering having flower seeds as unique save the date cards, buy the seeds at the end of the planting season when they have many on sale.

❀ If you would like to send a single chocolate as your save the date card, try making them yourself instead of buying them. Try the recipe on page 96 to make some delicious single truffles.

❀ Instead of buying separate pieces of card to make your invites with, buy a bulk amount of pre-folded cards in a multi-pack, which could work out cheaper and save you some valuable time.

❀ Look in interior design and DIY stores for free samples of wallpapers and fabrics, which you can scan and then use as backgrounds and patterns for your stationery.

❀ Now is the time to call in favours with any computer whizzes you may know. It will be a lot cheaper than going to a professional wedding company to get your stationery professionally designed and there's no reason why it won't look just as nice.

❀ Using finishing touches like some cheap ribbon or enclosing some dried petals is a great way to make a cheap invite look much more expensive.

❀ Making your own photo album will save you some pennies and possibly allow you to renegotiate your photography package to include something more valuable like a DVD of all the images.

❀ Printing out your stationery on a home printer is considerably cheaper than going to a professional printer. Buy glossy photo paper for a shiny look or matt for an un-shiny finish.

≈ Venues ≈

Choosing and booking a venue will be one of the first things you will do. But remember that your venue doesn't have to be a stately manor house or castle – it could be somewhere much closer to home. Many people these days opt to have their reception in a friend's or family member's house. However if you have your heart set on that amazing venue there's still some ways to cut your budget without cutting out your dream venue!

Budget busters

Here are some top tips for getting your dream venue, without spending a fortune…

❀ Many venues offer huge discounts for last-minute availability. Don't be scared by the 'last minute' term, as this can mean anything up to six months in advance. Obviously the nearer to the date you book, the cheaper you'll be able to get the venue – plus you'll be in a very good position to negotiate other extras such as food, drink and entertainment, etc.

❀ Book a weekday wedding, as these can be anything up to half the price of a wedding on a Saturday. People won't mind taking a day off work to attend, and if you hold it on a Friday people will have the weekend to recover!

❀ The off-peak season (October to March) is considerably cheaper than the summer and it will also have an impact on the pricing of other aspects of your wedding such as the flowers, entertainment, photography, etc. However remember to keep in mind that if you decide to have an autumn or winter wedding, its style will be considerably different from an outdoor summer wedding – though it'll be easier to predict the weather!

- If you or a family member has a large garden, why not hold the party there? Don't think that because it's 'just a garden' it won't be as special – decoration goes a long way.

- If nobody you know has a large garden (or doesn't want the hassle of holding a wedding reception), check out any local green areas where you could erect a marquee such as a local sports ground, school field or private land. As with any other venue you hire, make sure you always get a contract drawn up stating what time you have the area from and until, whose responsibility it is to clean up afterwards, permissions for third-party contractors and any other special requests you may have.

- It may be worth considering sharing your venue with another wedding party. Find out how much of a discount this would give you. As long as there are a number of different areas so both wedding parties can have areas of privacy, there shouldn't be a problem and could make financial sense.

- Ask your venue if you are allowed to provide your own food and drink. Some venues may let you do this while others won't be so keen as it can be a very profitable area for wedding venues. Some venues may let you provide your own drink for a 'corkage' fee. This is usually a small fee for opening and serving each bottle of wine. Even though this fee may seem a little cheeky, if you provide your own wine and champagne it can still work out to be a lot cheaper than buying the wine at the venue.

Real bride's tip

'My tip for other brides is try not to be influenced by other weddings you've been to. Each wedding is individual and just because Mrs X had a free bar doesn't mean you have to. Always do what you are comfortable with and don't get into debt by trying to keep up with someone else.'

CHOOSING A VENUE

Choosing where to get married may at first seem like a daunting task. There are literally hundreds of wedding venues across the country and when you open up the possibility of getting married abroad this becomes thousands. So where do you start? Here are a couple of questions to ask yourself to help you find that dream venue.

What's your budget?

Now's the time to find out if you're receiving any financial help from relatives. The conversation may be a bit awkward to bring up, but you definitely need to know so you can take everything into account when choosing a venue. There's no point in visiting venues that are way over your budget – you might fall in love with one of them that you could never afford. Be realistic. In six months' time, do you really want to be stressing over the price of things because you know you can't really afford it? By then it will be too late to change your mind, as you'll end up losing your deposit. It's easy to get carried away, but there are hundreds of wedding venues and there will definitely be a dream venue in your price range out there.

How far away do you want your venue to be?

Once you've decided on your budget, decide the distance you are prepared to make your guests travel. If you and your fiancé are not from the same area, would you like to have a venue somewhere in the middle, where you live now or perhaps where one of you grew up that's close to your heart? Ask yourselves if you think your guests would be prepared to travel and stay in a hotel, or perhaps you would like to get married abroad and make it a completely new and different experience for everyone? Are there any older relatives that you need to take into special consideration when thinking about travel arrangements?

Research

Once you've decided on your budget and an area where you would like to get married, it's time to start the fun job of researching venues. The easiest way to do this is on the internet. There are lots of good sites, which describe the venues available throughout the country and worldwide.

When you have a shortlist of venues, take advantage of the open days most venues offer and look around. Do you want to have the ceremony and reception at the same venue or would you like the reception to be somewhere else? Remember to take a camera and notepad along and jot down any thoughts or questions. Follow up your questions in an email later, after you have had time to go away and properly think about the venue. Whatever happens, try not to get carried away and book the venue on your first visit and definitely don't feel pressurised into signing anything straightaway!

QUESTIONS TO ASK POTENTIAL VENUES

When you are trying to choose a wedding venue, it can be easy to feel overwhelmed on the day of the visit and forget to ask important questions. Here are some key questions to take along and ask your venue.

- Is the venue licensed to hold civil ceremonies? If so, can they supply you with the contact details of the registrar.
- How many weddings do they hold at the venue on one day?
- What is the maximum number of people they can hold for the ceremony and reception?
- Are there different rooms available for the ceremony, wedding breakfast and evening reception?
- Is there any outdoor space?
- Is it possible to have a marquee if you wanted one?
- Would there be a room for the bride and groom to use throughout the day? You may want to touch up your hair and makeup during the day, or change into a different outfit for the evening.
- Is there a dressing room for the bride and the bridesmaids to use before the ceremony?
- Are children allowed at the venue?
- What time must the reception/music finish by?

Catering and decoration questions

- Do they insist on supplying all the catering, decoration, flowers, etc or are you allowed to provide your own or use contract third-party suppliers?
- If you want to do your own decoration what time are you able to access the venue from on the wedding day?
- Are you able to supply your own wine and champagne and is there a corkage fee for doing this?
- Until what time does their alcohol licence run and is it possible to get a late-night licence?
- Do they supply the wedding cake?
- Do they supply a cake stand and knife?

Extra questions

❀ Do they have recommended suppliers such as photographers, DJs, florists, transport companies, etc?

❀ Are there facilities available for connecting your own MP3 player for the music if you wanted to?

❀ Do they have a toastmaster available?

❀ Is there a PA system available to use for the speeches?

❀ What facilities are available if the weather is poor?

❀ Is confetti allowed to be thrown?

❀ Are candles allowed to be lit at the reception?

❀ Are there parking facilities available?

❀ Is there accommodation available at the venue or nearby for guests?

❀ Do they offer any discount for booking accommodation for the wedding?

❀ Will there be a dedicated member of staff available to you for the whole day?

TYPES OF VENUES

There are hundreds of different types of ceremony and reception venues for you to choose from, from the traditional to the more unusual and just bizarre! Here are a few suggestions:

❀ Manor house
❀ Church
❀ Castle
❀ Marquee
❀ Underwater (yes it really is possible!)
❀ Museum
❀ Hotel
❀ Sky diving
❀ Boats
❀ Restaurant
❀ Public house
❀ Town hall

❀ Library
❀ Golf course
❀ Hot air balloon
❀ Community hall
❀ Country club
❀ Public parks and gardens
❀ Zoo

MARQUEES

Marquees are a good cheaper alternative to an expensive indoor reception venue and these days they can be made to look as grand as any venue indoors. They come in all different sizes and the interior can be decorated to match your wedding colour scheme.

Different types of marquees

There are several different types of marquees available for hire, depending on where the marquee will be erected and the style you are going for.

❀ Framed marquees – These marquees have no centre poles or guy ropes, so they can be easily erected onto any surface (hard or soft) as they use weights instead of pegs. They are very stable and can span a wide area.

❀ Traditional pole marquees – These are attached to the ground by stakes and pegs so can only be erected on soft areas such as lawns or fields. Some people prefer the traditional poled marquees for their looks but they are less practical in terms of where they can be erected.

❀ Chinese hat pagodas – These are smaller modules, which can be easily joined to larger marquees to make areas of cover. They usually don't have side panels making it ideal for a smokers' area or an area of shade.

Inside a marquee

You can make the inside of your marquee look as plain or as grand as you like. There is the option of having an open grass floor but, if you think about all those ladies' heels getting stuck, you'll realise it's much better to have a hard floor especially if the weather is a little unpredictable. Some companies offer coconut matting and carpet at the cheaper end of the budget and hard wooden floors at the more expensive end. It is also possible to hire fancier floors for the dance area such as black and white squares. Just remember the fancier it looks, the pricier it will probably be, so think seriously about what's the most important thing to you.

Things to consider when hiring a marquee

If you're opting to hire a marquee rather than having your wedding in a purpose built building, then here's a few other areas that you may want to consider.

Parking

If the marquee will be erected in a garden or field, where will guests park their cars? If it's being erected in a private field, you should check with the owner of the field before you book the marquee whether vehicles are allowed on the grass or whether there is an area nearby that would be more suitable for parking. If the marquee is being installed at a house, is there a driveway or area nearby big enough to accommodate all the vehicles? The last thing you want on the day is to have neighbours dropping by complaining!

It is a good idea to include information about any parking arrangements on your invites (and don't forget to add it to the evening invites too).

Weather

While there's not much you can do about the weather (apart from crossing your fingers and hoping for the best), it is always a good idea to prepare for the worst case scenario. If you're getting married during the winter months, the chances are that a marquee may not be your number one choice so you probably won't need to prepare for snow. However there's as much chance that it will rain in August as in April. It's a good idea to ask your marquee supplier about the cost of hiring heaters should you get an awful weather forecast a few days before your wedding (or if you already know that it will be cold at the time of year you are having your wedding).

An idea for preventing your guests from getting too wet on the way into the marquee is to hire a marquee-roofed walkway, which can connect the car park or outer building to the main entrance of the marquee. A cheaper alternative to this is just to have a floor walkway, either by using plastic sheeting or carpet placed on the floor to the entrance of the main marquee. It won't have a roof on it, but it will protect people's shoes and long dresses from the soft (and perhaps wet) ground. This is something you can book (or even make yourself as a cheaper alternative) later on, when you know the weather forecast for your wedding day.

If it is a wet day remember to supply an umbrella bucket at the marquee's entrance to stop guests' wet umbrellas dripping onto the floor. You could even supply a few umbrellas yourselves, just in case it starts raining unpredictably.

Toilets

If your marquee will be at a venue where there's no access to an inside building, please don't forget to organise the lavatories! The cheapest lavatories to hire are portable toilets. While these may not be the prettiest in the world, here's a few ideas to make them look more attractive. You can also use these ideas to decorate toilets inside buildings even if you're not having a marquee.

- ❀ Add a few simple floral decorations inside the toilet.
- ❀ Use a couple of burning candles or incense sticks for a nicer smell.
- ❀ Perhaps you can add some humour to the inside of the toilets by putting up some funny photographs of the bride and groom and even some photographs of the guests. Make the toilets a talking point for all the right reasons!
- ❀ Don't forget to supply lots of toilet rolls and hand towels (the worse thing would be if you were to run out!). These can be presented in a decorated box or wicker basket with some flowers or ribbon attached. You could ask one male and one female friend to be in charge of making sure the toilets

look presentable throughout the day and night. It's probably not the best job in the world, but your friends really won't mind if it's one less thing you'll be worrying about on your wedding day.

If the thought of big grey portaloos fills you with dread, you could disguise their ugliness by hiring two smaller marquees to put them in. Just remember to make some signs to go outside that say which marquee is for whom.

An alternative to portable toilets is to hire luxury bathrooms, which are a little more expensive but usually include a dressing area such as a mirror for the ladies (important at a function such as a wedding for re-applying makeup). These luxury bathrooms look a lot nicer. They come in different colours and can range from one toilet in a block to several.

Remember that whatever lavatory area you hire, you will also have to use it. Trust me, going to the bathroom as a bride in a normal-sized toilet is a bit of an adventure (usually involving at least one other person to help you hold up your dress), so keep this in mind when choosing the size of your lavatories and whether it is important you have a mirror facility for checking and re-applying makeup. Also remember to take into consideration any special needs such as baby-changing facilities or any guests with disabilities.

Reception

Your reception will be as important to you as your ceremony. It is a reflection of your ability to throw a good party and you want your guests to have the best time they possibly can (and after all your months of planning, you will want to let your hair down too!).

DECIDING ON YOUR RECEPTION VENUE

First you need to decide whether you want your reception to be at the same venue as your ceremony or somewhere different, as your reception venue should be booked as soon as you have booked your ceremony venue.

If your ceremony and reception are at different venues, be sure to give your guests directions in advance, as well as any special parking instructions. Alternatively, you could provide transport between venues for guests who do not have access to vehicles. Hire a mini-bus, or an open top bus to add some adventure!

SELECTING THE RIGHT PACKAGE

When you book your reception venue you will probably be given a quote based on a package. There are usually different bands of packages, with the cheapest offering the least and the most expensive offering extra (or better quality) drinks and food. It's the hidden charges (or charges for extra items not included in your package) that increase your reception costs. Unfortunately many couples only find out about these extra charges after they have signed the contract with the venue, so make sure that you get in writing exactly what is included in your package before you sign or pay anything.

Here's a checklist of items that may be included in your package. If there's something on this list that isn't included in your package, be sure to get quotes from both your reception venue and third party suppliers for it. Always remember that it's definitely worth trying to negotiate.

- ❀ Welcome drink
- ❀ Welcome canapés
- ❀ Three course meal
- ❀ Table wine
- ❀ Table water
- ❀ Wedding cake
- ❀ Use of cake knife
- ❀ Toast master
- ❀ Toasting champagne
- ❀ Tableware (table cloths, chair covers, cutlery)
- ❀ Table flowers
- ❀ Table plan and place names
- ❀ Candles and holders
- ❀ Microphone for speeches
- ❀ DJ
- ❀ Bar set up
- ❀ Evening buffet
- ❀ Decorations (balloons, fairy lights, etc.)

ARRANGING THE SEATING PLAN

Surprisingly, the seating plan can be a very stressful part of the planning, especially if you or your fiancé have separated families. You should carefully consider whether you want to keep people in friends and family groups or mix everyone up. Remember you want your guests to have the best time possible.

Traditionally the bride and groom sit on a 'top' table with their parents, best man and chief bridesmaid facing all the other guests. However, these days it is not unusual for people to ignore tradition and let the bridesmaids and groomsmen sit with their friends and families, while people from separated families also have other seating arrangements. Another option that is becoming more popular for couples these days is not to have a top table but instead to sit at a normal table with the parents – or even to have a 'sweetheart' table where just the bride and groom sit. This allows the bride and groom to relax together for a little while before the evening reception starts and more guests arrive.

Here are some options for different family scenarios for top tables.

Key:

G = Groom   SF = Step father
B = Bride   M = Mother
CBM = Chief bridesmaid   SM = Step mother
F = Father

Traditional seating plan
CBM GF BM G B BF GM Best man

Bride's parents divorced and remarried
BSF CBM GF BM G B BF GM Best Man BSM

Groom's parents divorced and remarried
Best man GSM GF BM G B BF GM GSF CBM

If you want to mix guests around the tables it is always a good idea to have some kind of icebreaker to get them talking. One way of doing this is to have a scroll on each table with an introduction to each guest. Perhaps it could be an embarrassing or funny fact, or even a story of how the bride and groom know the guest. Any light-hearted humour will get everyone talking, even if they already know each other.

Naming the tables

When it comes to doing the seating plan, naming the tables can be a fun part of the job. Some couples stick to the traditional numeric naming, but why not inject some of your personality and memories into it? Here are some naming suggestions. You can even add photographs to illustrate the memories.

- ❀ The story of how you met
- ❀ Holidays
- ❀ Photos of both of you when you were younger
- ❀ Nights out
- ❀ Favourite memories
- ❀ Quotes
- ❀ Flowers
- ❀ Colours
- ❀ Where you got engaged
- ❀ Music idols
- ❀ Favourite sweets
- ❀ Different chocolates
- ❀ Animals
- ❀ Favourite holidays
- ❀ Songs
- ❀ Films
- ❀ The word 'love' written in different languages
- ❀ Honeymoon location
- ❀ Childhood memories

The advantage of personalising the table names is that you can link the theme to each table's centrepiece and to the favours. For example, if you choose your favourite sweets you can have a jar of these sweets on the table to double up as both the table name and the favours.

See the section on 'How to organise a table plan' in Chapter 1 for more information on seating plans.

Real bride's tip

'Don't forget to keep the children entertained at the wedding breakfast. We left three small goodie bags on the tables for each child – one for each course. They contained some colouring-in material, puzzles and some sweets which kept them amused and out of trouble!'

DECORATING YOUR RECEPTION VENUE

You should clarify with your venue to what extent they provide decorations. Do they provide candles for the tables or do you need to provide them? What about fairy lights or any other decorations such as balloons or lights for the dance area? If it's really important to you to have any of these, make sure you check with the venue in advance and don't wait for the big day to be surprised and possibly disappointed.

Whether your venue is old and traditional or funky and modern, amaze your guests with a touch of creativity and decorate it with some of these simple decorations. Even the simplest of decoration can a make a huge difference to the venue's ambience. Here are some simple ideas.

Candles

Tea lights and candles are an inexpensive way to give your venue a romantic ambient feel. You can buy them in bulk for very little and even buy scented candles, which will give off a lovely fragrance.

Lanterns

You can place lanterns in and around your venue and use them to create paths to link several different areas. See the Budget Busters on page 38 for more information on making homemade lanterns.

Fairy lights

Fairy lights can be wound round flower vases, added to tables or used to brighten up a dull area such as a concrete column. They are cheap and many people have them left over from Christmas so ask your family and friends if they have any before buying. You can also buy outside fairy lights to decorate bushes and trees.

> ### Real bride's tip
>
> *'We bought lots of decorations for our winter-wonderland themed wedding in the January sales when fairy lights were reduced in price.'*

Balloons

A few helium balloons, tied with ribbons and held down with weights, can make a huge difference to sparse, empty areas. You can also scatter a few balloons on the dance floor area, which is sure to be a hit with the children!

Dried petals

Scattered petals on the tables will add a romantic feel to the venue, especially if you are having minimal table decoration or plain tablecloths.

Chocolate fountain

If you really want to wow your guests with a fabulous centrepiece, hire a chocolate fountain with pieces of fruit and marshmellows. It can also double up as your dessert or replace a wedding cake. Just remember to watch your dress when you have some!

If the decorations are yours rather than the venue's make sure you organise for them to be collected the day after the wedding.

Budget busters

❀ Investigate hiring decorations rather than buying everything.

❀ Consider buying artificial flowers and topiary rather than fresh. That way you don't have to worry about the room needing to be a certain temperature to keep the flowers alive – plus they will last forever and you can keep them after the wedding.

❀ A cheap way to make a homemade lantern is to take a jam jar and wind some strong wire around the rim to create a handle. These can then be placed on the floor or even hung off trees.

Real bride's tip

'We bought some objects from home such as uplighters, candles and lamps to decorate our reception venue. It saved us from having to spend money on decorations that we would only use once.'

SPEECHES

Traditionally the speeches are given before, during and after the wedding breakfast with the groom, best man and father of the bride all giving speeches. These days not everyone sticks to this tradition and many brides and fathers of the groom also give speeches. There are in fact no rules in particular, just do what you feel comfortable with. If you would like to say a few words, but don't feel confident about making a speech, let your new husband say a few words from the both of you.

Top tips

❀ Don't be afraid to give the best man a few rules. If there's something that could ruin your day if he mentions (something rude or embarrassing if said in front of your friends and family) don't be afraid to tell him to avoid it. In most cases the best man will target the groom and leave the bride alone, but never leave it to chance!

- ❦ Traditionally the groom thanks the mothers or anybody else who has been especially helpful and gives out any thank you gifts, while the best man thanks the bridesmaids/flower girls/page boys and gives out those gifts.
- ❦ If you don't have a toastmaster to announce the speeches, appoint one of your ushers to take charge of announcing each person and help give a sense of order.
- ❦ Remember to organise a microphone and an area for the speeches. There is nothing worse than not being able to hear as that can lead to guests becoming bored.
- ❦ Give each speech a time limit and spread them out before, during and after the wedding breakfast.
- ❦ Props and pictures all help to keep guests interested during the speeches. If you want to do a slide show be sure to organise the equipment with the venue in advance and find a blank wall where it can be played in view of everyone.

AFTER DINNER ENTERTAINMENT

Children's entertainer

If you have children, or there's a large number of children attending your reception, it may be worth hiring a children's entertainer for after the wedding breakfast to keep them quiet. Anything from a balloonist to a Punch and Judy show should do the trick and stop them from getting too bored.

Fireworks

An expensive luxury, but definitely worth it if you have some money left in your budget. You will have to liaise carefully with your venue to find out if this is something that they can organise (and are allowed to do if the land is protected). It makes a great finale to the day, especially if you leave it as a surprise!

Chinese lanterns

A cheaper alternative to fireworks but just as much fun, Chinese lanterns also make a great finale to the wedding day. The idea is that you light the candle or fuel cell inside the lanterns and they fill up with hot air and float away. It makes a very romantic end to your special day.

Sparklers

If you can't afford fireworks or Chinese lanterns, sparklers make a fun second choice. You can buy sparklers in a range of different colours and there are even sparklers for indoor use if you don't have access to any outside space or if you are likely to have wet weather.

Balloons

Releasing helium balloons is a cheap and fun way to bring all the guests together during the day. You can add cards to the bottom of the balloons with your names and wedding date written on them.

Games

If you have a large outside space and want to keep the children entertained without paying for children's entertainers, hiring over-sized games such as Connect 4 and Noughts and Crosses is a good alternative. Children will love playing with the large games and I'm sure a few of the adults will join in too!

> *Real bride's tip*
>
> *Don't forget about your pets. We dressed our dog Jasper in a bow tie for the reception and he stole the limelight!'*

4 Getting married abroad

Nicer weather, less chance of rain, good food and a cheaper budget are all good reasons why people get married abroad. This mixed with the thought of a relaxing holiday before and after the big day makes it a very attractive proposal! But the thought of organising a wedding so far away can put some people off. As long as you get your paperwork in order beforehand and are prepared to put the time into organising the wedding, a wedding abroad can be more spectacular than stressful.

Budget busters

Save some money to put towards your wedding abroad by using these brilliant top tips.

❀ If you're lucky enough to get a great exchange rate around the time of booking your venue, take advantage of this. Try to pay more upfront than just the deposit in case the exchange rate goes down.

❀ Invest in a foreign currency card when the exchange rate is good. Just like a pre-paid card, you load money onto the card in the local currency and spend it abroad when you need to. These are becoming more widely available now and all have different restrictions, so research which one is best for your requirements.

❀ If you have a large number of guests travelling on the same plane, speak to the airline and see if you can negotiate a discount, or even a free upgrade for you and your groom.

❀ Hire one large mini-bus to transport your guests from the airport to your wedding location instead of using lots of separate taxis. It will be a great opportunity for everyone to meet each other before the wedding.

❀ If you have a lot of guests staying at one hotel, see if you can negotiate a discount or even a free room for your wedding night.

❀ Instead of asking for wedding presents, ask for local currency or experiences around your wedding venue. The experiences could be something such as a meal for the two of you or a spa treatment to help you both relax before the big day.

❀ Even if you are getting married abroad, you can still supply your own drink. When you do your reccy, speak to the local supermarket and see if you can negotiate a good deal for supplying you with a bulk amount. Just remember to check with your venue first whether they will charge a fee for this and how much.

❀ Organise welcome drinks for your wedding party in a local bar. Many local bars will be open to negotiating a good deal, especially if the guests will spend more money in there at another time. Perhaps they will even throw in a complimentary glass of champagne for you and your groom!

❀ If you would like to have favours for your wedding abroad, buy them from the local area instead of bringing them with you. You can negotiate a good deal from a local shop and make them something really unique.

❀ Buy your suncream and aftersun for your wedding abroad at the end of the summer season when many shops have sales. You will also be able to find other vital equipment you may need, such as fans, hats and sunglasses.

❧ Organising Your Paperwork

The paperwork for getting married abroad differs from country to country. It is possible to hire a company or tour operator to help you get all the paperwork sorted, but it's much cheaper if you put in a little hard work and put the money towards something more exciting!

By far the easiest place to get married is Las Vegas, whereas countries like France are much stricter and insist that you are a resident for 40 days prior to your wedding. The best place to contact for information on weddings abroad is your local town hall or the British embassy in your chosen country, who should be able to advise you on the paperwork you need for the particular country you are getting married in.

You may need some or all of the documents listed below, so make sure these are to hand and in order.

- A valid ten year passport
- A decree absolute if one or both of you is divorced
- A death certificate if one or both of you has been widowed
- Affidavit/statutory declaration stating you're both free to marry
- Parental consent if you're deemed underage in your chosen country
- Certificate of no impediment

When you are married, it is a good idea to obtain several copies of your wedding certificate as these can be hard to get hold of when you are back home.

❧ Pros and Cons of Getting Married Abroad

Pros

- You are more likely to have nicer weather.
- You are guaranteed to have a unique wedding day at a venue to which none of your guests have been before.

❀ You get the chance to have a relaxing mini-holiday before and after the wedding.

❀ You spend longer with friends and family.

❀ Weddings abroad are usually noticeably cheaper.

❀ You can double it up and take your honeymoon straight after.

❀ You can carry on the celebrations when you get home and have a party for the guests who couldn't attend.

Real bride's tip

'We made sure that we took one day out of the pre-wedding holiday to relax, just the two of us. It was nice to have the day to ourselves and not to have to worry about all the other guests.'

Cons

❀ You'll probably only be able to invite a small number of guests.

❀ Some guests may think attending will be out of their price range.

❀ You'll need to be organised and sort out your paperwork in advance.

❀ You'll have to research accommodation and be prepared to help your guests with questions about flights, transfers and things to see and do.

❀ If you don't speak the local language, the language barrier may become an issue. However most people who deal with events will probably speak English.

DO A RECCY

You've probably based your decision on where to have your wedding abroad by doing research on the internet or by word of mouth. It is a very good idea to visit your venue for at least a long weekend before booking it and parting with any cash. Photographs on the internet may have been manipulated to make a location look nicer than it actually does in real life and you want to make sure your wedding venue doesn't overlook a building site or something equally as bad.

By visiting the venue, not only will you get a better idea of how much you like it but it also serves as a great research trip to find out other deciding factors such as how easy and expensive it is to get from the airport to the area, names and prices of hotels and other things to see and do. Will there be enough in the area to keep your guests entertained before and after the wedding? How about very young and older guests, will it be difficult for them to get around?

Real bride's tip

If you're having your hair styled at a local hairdresser, book in your appointment as soon as possible – I found that they get booked up just as quickly as they do at home. I also picked up a few cards to give to some of my guests who had their hair styled before my wedding.'

INFORMATION FOR GUESTS

If you're going to get married abroad, you need to be that little bit more organised and let guests know far in advance what you are planning. This means that you should send out your save the date cards including the location details at least a year in advance so your guests have enough time to save up and plan for the flights and accommodation. See Chapter 1 for more information on save the date cards.

It is also essential that you send out a follow-up invitation with an information pack, which could alternatively be sent out a few weeks after the invitation once you know how many people are hoping to attend. The information pack should include information on the venue's location, the nearest airport, which airlines fly there, information on transfers (approximate prices are good to add if you can find them out), as well as hotels near the wedding/reception venue and a selection of things to do and see in the area before and after the wedding. If you already know the itinerary of the day it would be good to include it, as well as any events you are planning on having leading up to the wedding (such as a meal the night before), so guests know when they should arrive in the area.

Real bride's tip

'Before your guests arrive in the area, note down where the nearest banks, chemists, doctors, supermarkets, post offices and transport connections are. We gave our guests a local map and marked the locations on it. This saved us from having to say the same information over and over and our guests from getting lost.'

Real bride's tip

'We had an informal BBQ a couple of days before our wedding. It gave our guests the opportunity to meet each other and break the ice before the big day. Best of all, they could swap tips about what to see and do in the local area.'

Real bride's tip

'We thought of a plan for our guests for after the wedding reception had ended, as we knew they would want to carry on partying. We reserved an area in a local bar and supplied the first cocktail when they arrived, while we retired to our hotel room to relax after the day's events.'

Ideas for sending guest information packs

Invitation sent in a wallet with printed information

The only downside about this is that you need to have all the information before you send out the information wallets, as it can't be easily updated. Any updates would have to be printed out and re-sent.

Email

This is the cheapest way of informing guests. Just remember though that not everyone has access to email, especially any older relatives. Using email is a really easy way to contact people with any questions or updates, plus it's easy for guests to ask you questions.

Create your own wedding website

It is fairly easy these days to set up a wedding website for all your wedding information without having to be a website genius. You can add links to airlines, things to do and see and accommodation advice. You can also introduce guests to each other by posting their photographs along with short introductions to help people recognise each other while you are away.

There's lots of online sites that enable you to create your own wedding website. Some charge a small fee for your own personalised domain name while others are completely free. Creating a wedding website is a quick and easy way to share information with your family and friends and update any plans. Afterwards you can also share photographs and videos of the big day with people who couldn't attend as well as your memories from your honeymoon.

Here's a few wedding websites for you to look at and try. There are many more on the internet so do your research and find one which suits your needs.

- ❀ www.weddingpath.co.uk
- ❀ www.momentville.com
- ❀ www.gettingmarried.co.uk
- ❀ www.2haveand2hold.com
- ❀ www.mywedding.com

❀ www.projectwedding.com
❀ www.ewedding.com

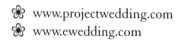

PACKING FOR A WEDDING ABROAD

The number one rule for packing for a wedding abroad is never, ever, pack anything in your suitcase that will ruin your wedding day if it's lost. I have heard so many stories about brides and grooms whose wedding days have been ruined by the wedding dress (which was packed in the main suitcase) getting lost or delayed. You need a bit of common sense! While in theory an airline should never lose your suitcase, why take the risk? It's taken you months of looking for that perfect dress and having alterations so that it fits you perfectly, so don't pack it in a suitcase just to be thrown around by an airline that might also lose it.

It is much easier and safer to buy a wedding travel box. These boxes are made to the standard size of hand luggage allowance and can be stored in the hand luggage compartment of your plane so it's never out of sight. You can order them online and as they come in many different pretty patterns you can use it afterwards to store your dress in. You should be able to leave your wedding box at your wedding shop and get them to pack your dress for you along with your veil, tiara and any other precious possessions your big day would be spoilt without.

If your shoes are expensive and you would be devastated if you lost them, try fitting them in your wedding box. If they won't fit, you could always ask a trusted member of your wedding party to bring them along as part of their hand luggage when they travel.

When you get your wedding dress out at the other end hang it up as soon as possible to let the creases drop out. If you have an ensuite bathroom try and hang it up near there, as the steam from the shower helps to remove the creases. Don't actually hang it in the bathroom though in case it drops into the bath, shower or, even worse, the toilet!

Every airline has a different baggage allowance so it's always a good idea to double check in advance what you are allowed to take with you – you don't want any last minute panics at the airport. If you are lucky enough to be travelling in premium economy, business or first class you may be able to store your dress and the groom's suit in another compartment, but it's always best to check. Look at your airline's website for more information.

Like your bridal dress and shoes you should encourage your groom to pack anything valuable and irreplaceable in his hand luggage such as shoes, ties or his wedding suit. These items will be hard to find abroad should his bag go missing and you don't want to ruin the beginning of your pre-wedding break panicking about missing items.

Real bride's tip

'I planned for every emergency I could think of. It's not as easy as going to your medicine cupboard when you are abroad and you don't want to turn up on your wedding day with a funny tummy!'

WEDDING ABROAD CHECKLIST

It's not possible when you're abroad just to pop to your drawer and get something last minute, so use this quick checklist to help you plan for any emergency.

- ❀ Hairdryer
- ❀ Hair curlers
- ❀ Hair straighteners
- ❀ Clips
- ❀ Hair bands
- ❀ Razors

- ❀ Nail varnish and nail varnish remover
- ❀ Safety pins
- ❀ White cotton and needle
- ❀ Small scissors
- ❀ Plasters
- ❀ Paracetamol
- ❀ Diarrhoea tablets and salts
- ❀ Insect repellent
- ❀ Insect bite cream
- ❀ Antihistamine tablets
- ❀ Moisturiser
- ❀ Suncream
- ❀ After sun
- ❀ Hand-held fan
- ❀ Umbrella (for sun and rain)
- ❀ Sun hat

Real bride's tip

'When you are relaxing in the days before your wedding be careful not to get sun burnt! When I wasn't sitting in the shade I made sure that I wore tops the same shape as my wedding dress so I didn't get any funny suntan lines.'

Real bride's tip

'Instead of stressing over whether I would get a tan for my wedding, I had a fake one done in England before I left. As well as being kinder on my skin I was able to relax and not risk getting sun burnt or any funny lines, which could have potentially ruined my wedding day!'

WEDDING INSURANCE

Whether you're getting married at home or abroad, I cannot recommend enough taking out wedding insurance. Thankfully only a small percentage of couples end up using their wedding insurance to make a claim, but those who do will tell you how it saved their wedding dream, especially when huge deposits have been lost. In these economic times no company is safe and you never know what will happen between the time you put down your deposit and your wedding day, so make sure you cover all possibilities by getting your wedding day insured.

When buying wedding insurance make sure you check and double-check exactly what is covered. You will probably need specific insurance for weddings abroad, so make sure you get the right insurance for your special day. You don't want to go to make a claim only to discover it was never covered in the first place.

THINGS TO CONSIDER WHEN GETTING MARRIED ABROAD

❀ Think about the groomsmen's suit hire. It will be expensive to hire suits to take abroad for a few days (plus there may be an extra insurance charge for doing so). These days you can buy good looking suits from high-street shops at a fraction of what they used to cost, and this usually works out to be cheaper than hiring a suit to take abroad. You can ask the men to pay for their suits or make a contribution towards them, or perhaps they can be a thank you present from you for all their help.

❀ Wedding insurance is a must have. You probably think that nothing will go wrong and you will probably be right. However, after all those months of planning and making everything exactly how you want it to be, insurance is a small price to pay for peace of mind that everything is covered should the worst happen.

❀ Do keep in mind that you are paying for the wedding in a foreign currency and you will work out your wedding budget on the current exchange rate. As the exchange rate can easily go up or down by the time your wedding day arrives, make sure you have budgeted for some contingency funds just in case.

❀ Even though you are more likely to have nicer weather abroad, it is still not guaranteed. Think about how you will feel if you travel all that way and get bad weather.

Real bride's tip

'Be prepared for rain. We had our hearts set on a sunny exotic wedding abroad but didn't have a plan (or clothes) in place for the rainy days!'

Transport

Transport to and from your wedding and reception venues can be an aspect you may forget to budget for. Some brides have their hearts set on arriving in a horse-drawn carriage, while others may not have given it much thought. Whatever your opinion, you will need to arrange something in advance and, the sooner you do it, the less you'll have to worry about nearer the wedding day.

THE NIGHT BEFORE THE WEDDING

Firstly, you need to decide where you and the groom will be staying the night before the wedding and with whom. Traditionally the bride gets ready with the bridesmaids and travels with them to the ceremony along with the father of the bride, while the groom gets ready with the best man and ushers. However, it's up to you who you would like to arrive with.

Next think about the distance from the place you are getting ready to the venue. If your venue is only five minutes away, you should avoid spending a fortune on expensive transport. Remember that you will also need to organise transport for everyone else getting ready with you as well as transport arrangements from the ceremony venue to the reception venue, if it's at a different location, and then from your reception venue to the hotel at the end of the night.

CHOOSING YOUR TRANSPORT

From the traditional to the wacky, there are lots of different options for your wedding day transport. Here are some ideas:

- Cars: Rolls Royce, Bentley, Porsche, Mercedes, Jaguar, Mini, Beetle, Limousine
- Motorbike and side-car
- Hot air balloon
- Helicopter
- Horse and carriage
- Red bus
- Mini bus
- Boat
- Bicycle
- Vespa

Budget busters

Here are some top tips for reducing your transport budget.

- Why spend money on transport if you can walk to the ceremony if it's not too far away? It will be fun with your bridesmaids and you will hear people congratulating you as you pass.
- Hire a car for the day and have one of the ushers drive you instead of hiring an expensive wedding car and driver.
- Use your own car or a family member's or friend's if somebody has one you like. You can decorate it with a ribbon and a 'just married' sign for after the ceremony.
- Fitting in all your bridesmaids and anyone else you want to arrive with into one vehicle will be cheaper than hiring several different vehicles. A mini bus or people carrier would be ideal. You can even decorate it to make it look more wedding themed.
- If you have your heart set on a mode of transport you really can't afford, ask somebody to pay for it as your wedding present.

Photography

Photography is one of the most important aspects of your wedding day. In years to come, your photos will carry the cherished memories of your special day and will be a keepsake to show your children and grandchildren. Therefore it is one of the areas you must get right. But with a little forward planning, it is still possible to cut the cost of your photo-graphy budget without losing the quality (and have some fun along the way!).

A LITTLE PLANNING GOES A LONG WAY

Before hiring a photographer, sit down with your fiancé and work out exactly what you want from your photographs – after all, once it's done there's no going back and re-doing it!

Style

What style of photography do you want? Do you want posed photographs, traditional, contemporary or more reportage (a photographer's term for 'caught in the moment'). Do you want black and white, sepia, colour or a mix of both? Black and white photographs tend to look more romantic but you may want to be reminded of certain elements of your wedding such as the colour of the flowers you chose or the bridesmaids' dresses. Don't be afraid to ask for a mix of both black and white and colour – it's not being greedy!

Film vs digital

Most photographers are now working in digital which has benefits for both the photographer and you. The photographer can immediately see the images and check if a shot has worked or needs to be re-taken. Also, if you want a mix of both colour and black and white he or she can use one camera and change the colour mode later, rather than bringing two cameras, one for colour film and one for black and white film. That means you could also have a say in which photographs are left in colour and which are made black and white.

Also, as the images are taken in digital format it's easy for you to get a CD or DVD of the photographs (rather than film images which would have to be scanned and then burned to a CD). However, some people still prefer the quality of images from film. They have a certain feel that sometimes can be lost in digital. So if you have a preference make sure you find out what medium your photographer will be using.

HIRING THE RIGHT PHOTOGRAPHER

Choosing a photographer to capture all the special memories of your wedding day is one of the most important decisions of your whole wedding planning. You want to hire someone experienced as well as someone you will feel relaxed with.

But finding the perfect photographer for your big day doesn't have to be stressful. Begin by researching on the internet and by word of mouth. Looking at online portfolios will instantly give you a feeling of whether their style is something you like or not. Once you've researched various prospective photographers, make a shortlist of three to four who you know are available for hire on your wedding day.

Next, arrange to interview and meet them in person. It is very important to meet the photographers in person rather than over the phone as this will give you an indication of whether you will feel relaxed with him or her on the big day. After all, you're going to be sharing one of the most important days of your life with this person so you want to feel comfortable with them.

QUESTIONS TO ASK PROSPECTIVE PHOTOGRAPHERS

As well as looking at the photographer's portfolio, remember to ask these key questions.

- How much wedding experience do they have?
- Have they photographed weddings at this venue before?
- What style of photography do they take?
- Do they use a digital camera or film?
- Do they take black and white, sepia or colour photographs and, if digital, can you have a say in which photographs are made black and white later?
- Can you give them a list of shots you want?
- Do they have an assistant?
- Will they be shooting the pictures personally or will it be another photographer on the day?
- How long do you have to make up your mind about choosing the photographs for the album?
- Are they insured?
- What happens if they are ill on the day?
- What packages can they offer?
- What is included in the price of the package?
- When will you receive the final images and album?
- Can you upgrade or swap out items?
- How many hours of photography are included in the package?
- Is a wedding album included in the price of the package?
- Do they have a contract?
- Can you view the contract?
- What are the payment terms?
- Do you have to pay a deposit?
- Are there any travel costs?
- What happens if you are not satisfied with the photographs?

'Make sure you are clear about exactly what is included in your photography package. I didn't realise prints of our photographs weren't included so afterwards we had to spend a lot of extra money having them printed up for our album.'

PLANNING YOUR PHOTOGRAPHS

On the day, there will be lots of people trying to have their photographs taken with you. While this is a lovely feeling, make sure you have given a list to your photographer of any particular people you want to have your photographs taken with, so you don't miss anyone out. It's helpful if you give your photographer a brief family tree (particularly if you have a divorced family) as this will help him or her to make sure you have the right set of parents/grandparents/siblings in each photograph.

Although posed photographs may not look like it, they usually take some time to set up so it's good to try and keep these kinds of photographs to a minimum. It's nice to have family photographs in the album but you don't want to spend the whole day having photographs taken – you really want to be able to enjoy spending time with your guests too.

It's a good idea to appoint two people (usually two of the ushers) who know the family to help the photographer find people and help set up the shots. You can prep them beforehand. Any help anyone can give you to make your day less stressful will also be welcome!

Other things to think about include whether there are any special objects you would like to capture in your photographs. For example, is there a particular piece of jewellery or family heirloom that has special meaning for you or your family? Or maybe it's something that somebody's made especially for the day, or those Manolos that you just had to buy for your special day? Think about the thank you cards in advance – maybe you'll want a special photograph of something in particular for someone.

Once you've selected your photographer, you are likely to have two or three meetings before the big day. At one of these meetings, you'll probably discuss areas at your venue for photographs. Before you meet up with your photographer, it is a good idea to go to your venue and scout out any areas you are particularly fond of and note them down. You could even take a few snaps to show your photographer in case he or she does not know the areas you are talking about. While the photographer is more experienced about which areas would make nice backgrounds/shots, you shouldn't be shy in giving some direction. Just remember to keep in mind that the grounds can change depending on how far in advance you go. For example, if you visit in the summer and your wedding is in the autumn, those lovely flowers will probably have changed by your wedding date.

Real bride's tip

'Some of my most favourite photographs were actually from before the ceremony, of me and my bridesmaids getting ready. I didn't actually think I would cherish these memories as much as I do now and I'm so glad the photographer suggested to capture those moments.'

Budget busters

Here are some top tips for reducing your photography budget … and for having some fun on the day!

❀ If you have a friend or relative who's good at photography, why not ask them to take some photos instead of hiring a photographer? You can easily hire a good camera and tripod for the day from a high-street photography shop. Before the big day, you could have a test shoot at the venue to get them used to taking photos there and also to give them some ideas about what you want.

❀ All photographers will give you a quote based on a package. These packages differ greatly and some will include the price of a photo album displaying your photographs. If you're not too bothered about doing your own album why not lose this from the package and re-negotiate the price to save a few pennies.

❀ Consider swapping the photo album for something more useful like a DVD of all the pictures so you can print your photos yourself. This will save some money after the wedding as some photographers charge a lot for prints.

❀ Why not hire a photographer for just the ceremony instead of both the ceremony and reception. Most of the family photos will be taken after the ceremony before the reception so you will already have these, then ask one or two of your friends or ushers to take photos during the reception.

❀ Let your guests help you be the photographers by leaving disposable cameras on the tables. A lot of wedding shops sell them, however you'll find them at much cheaper prices in high-street supermarkets. If these cameras don't look as pretty as the ones in the wedding shops, simply pop them in small, coloured bags or wrap them up in tissue paper to match your colour scheme. The guests will have lots of fun using them – just remember to appoint an usher to collect them at the end of the evening.

❀ Hire a photo booth, instead of an evening photographer. This is a fun way of capturing everyone at the wedding and will certainly be a talking point!

❧ Most of your guests will take their own photographs at your wedding and some of these will be surprisingly good (one of my favourite photos was in fact taken by my mum and not the professional photographer!). However a lot of these photos you may not get to see, so why not leave blank CDs with self-addressed envelopes on your guests' tables with notes asking them to send you copies. They really won't mind and it'll be fun to see their view of your wedding day!

❧ In theory a film of the wedding day and reception seems like a good idea. And it is. It's lovely to hear the music playing and hear the speeches, which you can't in photographs. However in reality you'll probably only watch your DVD a couple of times – it's just nice to know it's there. Therefore avoid spending a lot of money on it. You'll probably have a family member or friend who is capable of filming the day for you and save you some more pennies to put towards your honeymoon.

❧ Print your photographs out on a home printer, rather than having the photographer supply them as part of their package. You will have so many to choose from and it's likely there'll only be one or two which you want to have enlarged.

❧ Have all your photographs printed as one large montage instead of lots of individual photos. You can then get this mounted in a frame instead of placing each one individually into an album – saving both time and money.

Real bride's tip

'To save money we didn't have the photographs printed as part of our package and instead got a DVD of all the images. Not only did this save us cash, but it allowed us to pick just our favourite images out of the whole day.'

7

Music

MUSIC FOR THE CEREMONY

Whether you hire live music or a DJ, or use CDs or a MP3 player, music is a must for both your ceremony and reception. Guests generally arrive at the ceremony venue up to 45 minutes before it starts and you need to decide whether you want any music playing while they are waiting. This could either be live music such as a string quartet or harpist, or a CD of classical music.

Music choices for the moment you walk down the aisle also need to be carefully considered. Some people stick to traditional music, while others prefer something more unique and personal. The choice is completely up to you; there's no right or wrong decision. Here are some suggestions of the most popular music for the ceremony.

PRELUDE

For the guests' arrival at the ceremony venue:

- ❀ Ave Maria
- ❀ Greensleeves
- ❀ Prelude in C
- ❀ Canon in D
- ❀ Beethoven's Fifth Symphony
- ❀ Air on the G string

- Minuet in G
- The Gift Without a Bow
- A Father's Song
- Someone to Watch Over Me

THE PROCESSIONAL

For the bride's entrance with the bridesmaids:

- The Wedding March
- Air on the G String
- Spring (from Vivaldi's Four Seasons)
- Arrival of the Queen of Sheba
- A Midsummer Night's Dream
- Processional in D

WEDDING HYMNS

- All Things Bright and Beautiful
- Amazing Grace
- Give Me Joy In My Heart
- Make Me a Channel of Your Peace
- Morning Has Broken
- O Worship the King
- The Lord's My Shepherd

THE DEPARTURE

For the bride and groom's departure from the ceremony after getting married:

- Alla Hornpipe
- Wedding March
- Canon in D

❀ Music for the Royal Fireworks
❀ Finale from Symphony No. 1

MUSIC FOR THE RECEPTION

As well as music for the ceremony, music for the reception should also be carefully considered. It's important to get your party started and create the right atmosphere for you and your guests to be able to relax in.

BAND VS DJ

For the reception, many people find it hard to decide whether to hire a band, DJ or both. Think about the type of atmosphere you want to create, as there are many types of bands out there from jazz to pop music. Here are a few questions to help you decide.

❀ Do you want music played during the welcome drinks and the wedding breakfast or only later on during the evening reception?
❀ Is it important to you to have live music?
❀ Do you want your first dance to be to live music? Keep in mind that the live version may be a little different to the CD version.
❀ Is it important to you to have modern day pop songs?
❀ Does the band or DJ you are thinking about hiring have the type of tracks you want to play? There's no point in hiring a DJ that doesn't have any of the type of music you like.

FIRST DANCE

Whether you have a dance already rehearsed or you are doing it off-the-cuff, your first dance will probably be a nerve-wrecking occasion. You want it to go as smoothly as possible, so here are a couple of top tips.

If the band or DJ is providing the music for the first dance, make sure this is the same version that you want. If the version you want is slowed-down or a unique version, make sure you provide it in case the band or DJ cannot find it.

Some couples prefer to dance the whole of their first dance by themselves (especially if they have a dance routine rehearsed), while others prefer for other guests to join in. If you would like other people to join you, let one or two couples know beforehand so they will join in and encourage others to follow.

You may already have a song that you call your own, but if not then here's some romantic inspiration for your first dance choice:

❀ Amazed – Lonestar
❀ At Last – Etta James
❀ Can't Help Falling in Love – Elvis
❀ Can't Take My Eyes Off You – Andy Williams
❀ Chasing Cars – Snow Patrol
❀ Crazy For You – Madonna
❀ Endless Love – Diana Ross and Lionel Ritchie
❀ Everything – Michael Bublé
❀ Fly Me To The Moon – Frank Sinatra
❀ Have I Told You Lately – Rod Stewart
❀ It Had To Be You – Harry Connick Jr
❀ (I've Had) The Time of My Life – Bill Medley and Jennifer Warnes
❀ I Will Always Love You – Whitney Houston
❀ Let's Stay Together – Al Green
❀ Let There Be Love – Frank Sinatra
❀ She's The One – Robbie Williams
❀ That's Amore – Dean Martin
❀ The Look of Love – Dusty Springfield
❀ Over the Rainbow – Eva Cassidy
❀ Unforgettable – Nat King Cole
❀ What a Wonderful World – Louis Armstrong
❀ When a Man Loves a Woman – Percy Sledge

PARTY MUSIC

Having an empty dance floor at your reception is every bride's nightmare! Make sure you plan ahead and collect track suggestions from your guests so this doesn't happen at your reception. Think about the type of guests you have coming and play something for everyone. Here are some popular music tracks to get your party started.

- 9 to 5 – Dolly Parton
- Addicted to Love – Robert Palmer
- Another One Bites the Dust – Queen
- Baby Got Back – Sir Mix-a-Lot
- Beautiful Day – U2
- Billie Jean – Michael Jackson
- Build Me Up Buttercup – The Foundations
- Car Wash – Rose Royce
- Chain Reaction – Diana Ross
- Come on Eileen – Dexy's Midnight Runners
- Copacabana – Barry Manilow
- Dance the Night Away – Mavericks
- Dancing in the Street – Martha Reeves and The Vandellas
- Dancing Queen – Abba
- Do You Love Me (Now That I Can Dance) – The Contours
- Don't Stop Me Now – Queen
- Footloose – Kenny Logans
- Girls' Just Want to Have Fun – Cyndi Lauper
- Grease Megamix – John Travolta and Olivia Newton-John
- Holiday – Madonna
- Hungry Eyes – Eric Carmen
- I Wanna Dance With Somebody – Whitney Houston
- I'm In the Mood for Dancing – The Nolans

- I'm Still Standing – Elton John
- I'm Your Man – Wham!
- Is This the Way to Amarillo – Tony Christie
- (I've Had) The Time of My Life – Bill Medley and Jennifer Warnes
- Karma Chameleon – Culture Club
- Love Shack – The B-52's
- Macarena – Los del Rio
- Mamma Mia – Abba
- Mustang Sally – The Commitments
- New York, New York – Frank Sinatra
- Oh, Pretty Woman – Roy Orbison
- Sex Bomb – Tom Jones and Mousse T
- The Shoop Shoop Song (It's in His Kiss) – Cher
- Stayin' Alive – Bee Gees
- Stuck in the Middle With You – Stealers Wheel
- The One and Only – Chesney Hawkes
- Thriller – Michael Jackson
- The Time Warp – Damian
- Twist and Shout – The Beatles
- Wake Me Up Before You Go-Go – Wham!
- Y.M.C.A. – Village People
- Young Hearts Run Free – Candi Staton

Real bride's tip

We left music request cards on the tables at the wedding breakfast. Our guests filled them in with their choices and gave them to the DJ. It was great that the guests could have a say in which music was played and our dance floor was packed!'

Budget busters

Here are some top tips for reducing your music budget.

❀ Instead of paying out for live music before and during the ceremony, play a classical CD instead.

❀ Consider hiring a jukebox for the evening's music instead of a DJ. This will not only give your guests full control over the music they listen to, but it will also be cheaper than hiring a DJ.

❀ Another even cheaper alternative to hiring a DJ is to hook up your MP3 player to a speaker system. You can ask your guests for song requests on your invitations and load them onto your MP3 player in advance. Just make sure to check with your venue that they have the facilities available to do this.

Flowers

Flowers are an important part of your wedding day. At first they can seem to be an unnecessary luxury, however don't under estimate the ambience flowers can bring to an occasion. By following a few simple tips you can still add a touch of floral ambience without breaking the bank.

Budget busters

Here are some top tips for getting the floral decorations you want without spending a fortune.

- ❀ Try to avoid holding your wedding around any nationally celebrated events such as Christmas, Easter or Valentine's Day, when the florists will be extra busy and the cost of flowers will be higher than at other times of the year.
- ❀ Keep your bouquets to a minimum. You could have one for the bride and then let the bridesmaids hold a single flower instead of a bouquet.
- ❀ Another cheaper alternative to bridesmaids' bouquets is to have wrist or pinned corsages. These will add a simple sophisticated look to your wedding. You can even have fun with your bridesmaids by making these yourselves.
- ❀ Make the effort and visit a flower market for your wedding flowers instead of a florist who will add a mark-up to any flowers they supply. Make sure you can visit the market a few

weeks in advance to see if they stock the flowers you want and don't feel shy about talking to the stallholders and negotiating a good deal.

❀ It's still popular to have buttonhole flowers for the groomsmen and guests. Think about whether you really want them, as this is an area where you can save some money (and time). If you do still want them, get your bridesmaids round and try making them yourselves. Make sure you do a trial run before the big day though!

❀ Instead of having large expensive fresh flower table decorations on every table at the wedding breakfast, pot plants make a great alternative. They are fun and different and can represent the table names.

❀ Consider growing your own flowers for your wedding bouquet and table decorations instead of buying them. This works particularly well if you're having potted table centrepieces instead of fresh cut flowers.

❀ Another alternative to fresh flower table decorations is to swap them for candles and dried petals.

❀ If your ceremony will be at a different venue to the wedding reception, ask if you're allowed to take the floral arrangements with you. Even though this may take some careful arranging (you will need to put someone in charge of carefully transporting them), it could save you some money on the reception flower budget.

❀ Instead of buying expensive flower vases (or even hiring them from a florist), hit the high street and supermarkets and find cheap vases. There's no reason why all the vases have to match and for a fun alternative think about using jam jars, silver boxes and fish bowls, which all can be decorated with ribbons, stones and candles.

FLOWERS IN BLOOM

Before you have your heart set on particular bouquet or floral arrangement, it's important to work out what flowers will be in season when you get married. The cost of your flowers could rise significantly if you really want a flower that is not in bloom when you get married, so always check before committing to an arrangement. The following are popular wedding flowers and their seasons.

Spring

Muscari
Colour: Shades of blue, violet and white
Shape: Clusters of tiny tubular flowers

Hyacinth
Colour: Various
Shape: Spikes of tubular flowers that often have a strong scent

Lilac
Colour: White and lilac
Shape: Small star shape flowers on tall woody stems

Tulip
Colour: A range of colours to suit any wedding colour scheme
Shape: Trumpet-shaped flowers

Lily of the Valley
Colour: White
Shape: Small bell-shaped buds on short delicate stems

Summer

Peony
Colour : White, pale or deep pink, pale peach and maroon
Shape: Big flower heads

Sweet Pea
Colour: Pink, cream and mauve
Shape: Short thin stems of petals

Hydrangea
Colour: White, pink, blue, green, red/brown
Shape: Star shaped flowers in wide heads

Sweet William
Colour: Various colours in a variety of shades, from white to deep red
Shape: Lots of tiny flowers, which form a dense head

Delphinium
Colour: Blue, purple and white
Shape: Towering spikes of flowers

Agapanthus
Colour: Blue and white
Shape: A cluster of funnel-shaped flowers on a tall stem

Autumn

Zinnia
Colour: Yellow, red or orange often with black stripes
Shape: Large, flat-headed blooms

Gladioli
Colour: Pastel colours of red, purple and orange
Shape: Long stems of at least ten funnel-shaped flowers

Sedum
Colour: Shades of pinky-brown with green stems
Shape: Clusters of star-shaped flowers

Hypericum
Colour: Yellow flowers; berries in red, brown and orange
Shape: Cup-shaped flowers

Nerine
Colour: Hot or pale pink
Shape: Slender curled petals

Winter

Hellebore
Colour: A range of colours to suit any wedding colour scheme
Shape: Trumpet-shaped flowers

Anemone
Colour: Red, purple, pink or white with a black centre
Shape: Large, flat flower heads

Ranunculus
Colour: White, yellow, pink, red or orange
Shape: Bowl-shaped flower heads

Eucharis
Colour: White
Shape: Up to four daffodil-shaped flowers at the end of each stem

Amaryllis
Colour: White, pale pink, burgundy or crimson
Shape: Huge, open trumpets

Available all year round

Rose
Colour: A range of colours to suit any wedding colour scheme
Shape: Variety of sizes available

Freesia
Colour: Various colours
Shape: A tiny, delicate looking flower

Orchid
Colour: White
Shape: Exotic flowers ranging from small Singapore Orchids to much larger versions

Gerbera
Colour: Many vivid colours available
Shape: Large daisy-like blooms

Anthurium
Colour: White, pink or red
Shape: Waxy upside down heart-shaped flowers with protruding spike

Longi Lily
Colour: White with yellow centres
Shape: Trumpet-shaped flower head

Calla Lily
Colour: Pink, cream, purple, orange and yellow
Shape: Funnel-shaped flower

Carnation
Colour: Various colours, including some two-tones
Shape: Large flower heads

FOLIAGE

Foliage is a good and cheap way of bulking out a floral arrangement. Most foliage is available all year round. Here's a quick guide to the most popular.

- Ferns – A number of varieties are available, such as Asparagus and Bird's Nest, which add movement to a design.
- Grasses – Bear, Steel, etc. Suitable for all sorts of arrangements.
- Baker's Leaf – A commonly used foliage which is mainly used to cover exposed foam and give more volume to an arrangement.
- Ruscus – Either soft or hard. Soft Ruscus is very floaty. Both varieties are long stemmed.
- Bupleurum – Long and thin leaves that resemble fennel. Adds colour and shape to a flower arrangement.
- Monstera Leaf – Monstera leaves are big, wide and heart-shaped.
- Eucalyptus – Several varieties available with varying colours and leaf shapes. It has a wonderful scent.
- Hypericum – These berries are perfect for adding a touch of colour to an arrangement. They range in colours from orange to brown/red.
- Molucella – Otherwise known as the Bells of Ireland, this is a green flower rather than foliage, but it bulks out a floral arrangement in the same way.
- Variegated Ivy – Commonly used in arrangements as well as bridal bouquets. It matches perfectly with roses. Its structure is like vine and when used correctly can create beautiful curvy lines.
- Dusty Miller – Silver/grey in colour with a velvety texture. It matches well with pink roses.
- Twigs – Rose Hip, Pussy Willow and Dogwood stems all add a unique twist to a floral decoration.

MEANINGS OF FLOWERS

Traditionally, different flowers have different meanings. Perhaps you would like to choose your wedding flowers based on one of these.

- Bluebell – Everlasting love
- Camellia – Perfect loveliness
- Daisy – Innocence
- Gardenia – Joy
- Honeysuckle – Devoted affection
- Hyacinth – Playfulness
- Ivy – Fidelity
- Jasmine – Grace and elegance
- Lily of the Valley – Happiness
- Orchid – Delicate beauty
- Rose (white) – Purity
- Rose (red) – Passionate love
- Stephanotis – Good luck
- Sweet Pea – Shyness
- Violet – Faithfulness

KEEPING YOUR WEDDING FLOWERS

A nice memento from your wedding day is to keep flowers from your wedding bouquet. A good way to do this (without letting them go crispy in a box somewhere) is to press and frame them. You can then hang your flowers up in your house or alternatively press and use them to create the thank you cards.

How to press flowers

1. Make sure your flowers are dry but not wilted. Usually only the flowers are pressed (and not the stem), but it's up to you if you want to press some of the foliage as well.

2. Remove the petals from the thick centre core, pressing the flowers flat with your fingers.

3. Using a heavy book, insert a folded facial tissue or thin piece of paper within a spread of pages. Place the petals and flowers on the tissue inside the fold. Skip a few pages and repeat the process. The reason for using a tissue or thin piece of paper is so that you can easily transfer the flowers once dry.

4. After a day or two transfer the tissue along with the flower to another heavy book. This is to remove moisture from the plant. Leave the flowers in the book for another two to three days or until completely flat. After this, remove them from the tissue paper and mount onto acid free paper in a picture frame. You will be able to hang this in your house for an everlasting memory of your wedding flowers.

Real bride's tip

'We used the bridesmaids' bouquets as thank you presents for our mothers. It saved us from spending extra money on more bouquets and, best of all, wasting the gorgeous bridesmaids' bouquets.'

BUTTONHOLES

Making your own buttonholes will not only be incredibly satisfying but will also save you a lot of money. Start to practise making them a few weeks before you need to make the final ones, so you know how much time to allow and whether you like them. At first they may seem slow to make, but after a few you'll soon whizz through them and you'll find them really easy!

Traditionally the groom's buttonhole is made up from the same flowers as the bride's bouquet and may be a different flower and colour from the other buttonholes to distinguish him from the rest of the group. Alternatively, you can use any flowers to make your buttonholes. Flowers such as carnations, daisies, roses, gardenias and calla lilies all make ideal choices. Keep the flowers in the fridge so that they stay fresh until they are needed and in a dark place if you want to avoid the blooms opening further. Alternatively artificial flowers also make a good choice for buttonholes if you prefer.

To keep the flowers looking their best you should try and make the buttonholes no more than one to two days before your wedding day and store them in a cool place to stop them from wilting. Obviously, if you use artificial flowers you can make them further in advance and store them in a box to save them from getting dirty or damaged.

A simple step-by-step guide to making buttonholes

For each buttonhole you will need:

> 1 rose (or flower head of your choice)
> 5 rose leaves
> Flower tape
> Heavy gauge stub wire
> Silver rose wire

1. The first step is to wire the leaves. Take a single leaf and a length of rose wire. Thread the wire through the main vein at the back of the leaf about two thirds of the way up.
2. Bring the ends of the wire back down towards the stem and twist one around the stem and the other end of wire.
3. Repeat this with all the other leaves except the fifth leaf. For the fifth leaf just go as far as step 1.
4. Using two of the wired leaves and the fifth leaf, make a three-leafed sprig. Place the three leaves together with the fifth leaf placed on the right hand side. Then twist the wires of the fifth leaf around all three stems so that the leaves are joined together.
5. Now you have to wire the flower head. Cut the stem about 1.5 cm below the calyx (the green bottom of the flower head). Push the stub wire up the stem and into the seed box. Then push a rose wire through the flower head at its base.

Step-by-step guide to making buttonholes

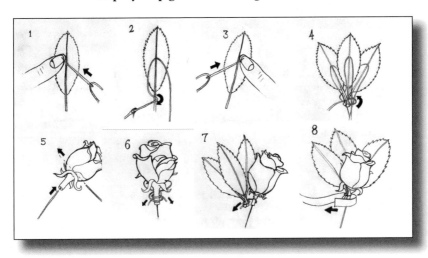

6. Gently bring the ends of the rose wire down and wrap one of the ends around the other one and the stub wire binding them together.
7. Place the wired rose on top of the three-leafed sprig and wire together.
8. Tape the wired rose and three-leafed sprig together then finish off by taping the two single leaves underneath the flower. Gently bend the wires so that the leaves sit neatly in place.

HAND-TIED BOUQUETS

Bouquets should be made the day before your wedding so they look their best on your wedding day. You can use these simple instructions to make both your bridal and your bridesmaids' bouquets though, for a really easy floral arrangement, give your bridesmaid a single flower to hold.

You can also make a bouquet using artificial flowers, which will allow you to keep your bouquet after the wedding. Another advantage of using artificial flowers is that you can make your bouquets weeks in advance without the fear of your flowers wilting and you can take your time to get them looking perfect.

> ### *Real bride's tip*
>
> *'Don't disregard using artificial flowers too quickly. I thought that they would look cheap and tacky, but I found some good quality ones made from silk which looked very realistic. I now have them in a vase in my house as a constant reminder of my wedding day and I even lent them to my sister for her wedding.'*

A simple step-by-step guide to making a hand-tied bouquet

This bouquet uses lilies and roses, but you can adapt it to the flowers of your choice.

You will need:

3 stems of lilies with a mixture of both buds and flowers on each
6 roses
Gyposophila or wax flowers
Some foliage like bear grass and eucalyptus
Twine
Scissors
Secateurs
Ribbon

1. Prepare your flowers. Remove the thorns from the roses and the lower leaves from the stems. Clean the stems and remove any dirt. Remove the stamens from the centre of the lilies as they could leave a bright yellow stain on your dress.
   Next take a small bunch of eucalyptus and bind together with a long piece of twine.
2. Lay one of the lilies on top of the eucalyptus vertically. Then take two stems of gypospohila or wax flowers and place the first on a diagonal going from left to right.

3. Holding the bouquet with your left hand, use your right hand to place the other stem of gyposophila behind the bouquet so that it goes from right to left.

4. Use a length of twine to bind the stems together to hold them in place.

5. Keep repeating the process, adding a mixture of foliage and flowers by placing a stem across the front diagonally from left to right then a stem at the back from right to left. This process builds up the bouquet to create a dome shape, which will make it easy for you to hold.

6. After adding each layer of flowers and foliage, rotate the bouquet to make sure it looks good from all angles. Once you are happy with the bouquet, tie the twine into a knot. Then using cutters, trim the stems into one neat length.

Tie a piece of ribbon round the stems to hide the twine. The ribbon can be held in place with a pearl-ended pin or tie into a bow. Store your bouquet in a vase in a cool place until your wedding day.

Step-by-step guide to making a hand-tied bouquet

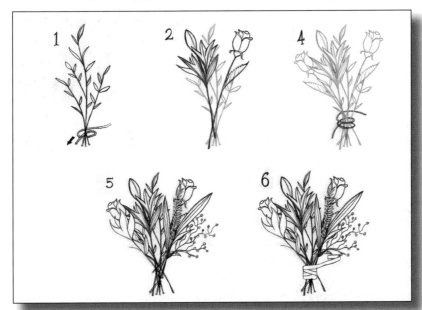

FLORAL TABLE CENTREPIECES

Flowers are a popular choice for centrepieces as they add colour and fragrance to a room. There are several ways of displaying a flower centrepiece – here are a few ideas.

Floating flowers

This is a really easy centrepiece to get right and it works well with large flat flower heads.

Step-by-step guide to making a floating centrepiece

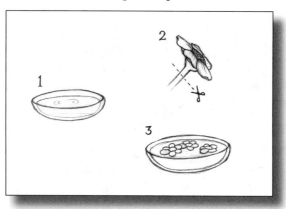

1. Buy or hire some large glass bowls – any shaped bowl works well, particularly shallow or fishbowl shapes.
2. Next, using scissors cut the heads off the stems to leave you just the flower heads.
3. Fill the bowl up half way with water and place the flower heads on top with the centre of the flowers facing upwards. To make this floral decoration more interesting, add some floating candles, pebbles or a touch of food dye to the water to match your colour scheme.

Glass vase

Another easy way to display floral decorations on the table is to place them in a glass vase. It is best to choose tall vases with long stemmed flowers so you don't block out guests' views of one other and make the table anti-social. Simply place your chosen flowers into a vase and add some foliage. Remember that the wider the vase, the more flowers you will need otherwise the vase could look empty and disappointing – so if budget is vital choose a thin vase! You could opt for a coloured vase to match your colour scheme and even decorate the vase with a piece of ribbon, fairy lights or scattered petals round the bottom.

Cut flower display

The most popular way of displaying your own floral decorations on the tables is by using an oasis brick (a foam green brick used by florists) to hold the flowers in place. This is a really easy instrument to use for gradually building up your arrangement. For a romantic evening look try inserting a candle into the centre.

Step-by-step guide to making a cut flower centrepiece

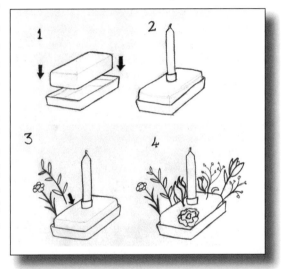

A simple step-by-step guide to creating your own table centrepiece

For each centrepiece you will need:

Tray
Oasis brick (wet rather than dry)
Candle inserted into a candle holder
Your chosen flowers
Foliage – e.g. gyposophila, bear grass, eucalyptus

1. Cut the oasis brick to fit the size of the tray. Soak the brick thoroughly in water. This will water your flowers and keep them looking fresh.
2. Insert the candle into the centre of the oasis brick.

3. Start inserting short sprigs of foliage to the sides of the brick. Continue to do this to gradually build up the sides.

4. Start adding your main flowers into the brick to build up the main arrangement. Remember to keep in mind that the arrangement will be seen from all angles, so keep rotating it to make sure it looks good from all sides.

5. Keep adding the flowers to cover the brick completely, alternating between the main flowers, small flowers and the foliage. You are aiming to create a soft looking arrangement.

To keep your flowers looking their best you should make this arrangement just a day or two before your wedding day so that the flowers don't wilt. You can also use artificial flowers to create this centrepiece. If you are using artificial flowers, you do not need to wet the oasis brick and your arrangement will be a cherished memory long after your wedding day has passed.

Food and drink

Food and drink will be one of the most expensive areas of your wedding budget. However with some careful planning it is possible to lower these costs without compromising the quality.

FOOD SUPPLIERS AT VENUES

First of all you need to find out if it's compulsory that your wedding venue provides the food and drink or if you're allowed to provide your own (including hiring third party caterers). Hopefully this is something which you would have found out and considered before booking your venue, especially if your budget relies heavily on you supplying your own food and drink.

Budget busters

Here are some top tips for reducing your food and drink budget.

❀ Providing your own food (or getting family or friends to help you make it) will reduce costs significantly and help to make the day feel more personal. Plus all your guests will love the home cooking!

❀ Consider growing your own vegetables for the meal. You could even put this on the menu.

❀ Think about having a light afternoon tea, instead of having a late sit-down meal. People will generally want to eat and drink less in the afternoon than later on.

❀ Stick to foods that are less expensive to find and supply. Food such as lobster, beef tenderloins and prawns are usually more expensive and should be avoided. If you really want to serve this kind of food, consider serving it as smaller dishes such as canapés or starters.

❀ If your heart is set on a sit-down meal, design your menu around as few courses as possible.

❀ Cut the costs on dessert by serving the wedding cake instead.

❀ Consider having a buffet. Not only will this offer guests a wider selection of foods to choose from (especially fussy eaters), but it will also cut out waiting costs as guests will serve themselves.

❀ If you are going to provide the food and drink yourself, it will be significantly cheaper to buy what you need in bulk from a warehouse instead of at a supermarket. Just remember that you may need to hire crockery, utensils, serving ware and glasses.

❀ If you are having a summer wedding, have a BBQ instead of a sit-down meal. This will be a lot cheaper as guests will only eat the food that they want – which is usually less than a three-course meal.

❀ If you are supplying the wine, you may still be charged a 'corkage' fee by your venue. This is a fee for opening and serving each bottle of wine. It may seem a little steep, however it can still work out to be a lot cheaper than buying the drinks from the venue. The rules on corkage fees differ from venue to venue, but the same fee may also be applied to other drinks you supply yourself such as beer, spirits and non-alcoholic drinks. Ask your venue whether you could get the corkage waived or at least discounted if someone (such as the ushers) opens and pours the wine in advance.

> ❀ Swap the toasting champagne for Cava, Brut or Prosecco. These alternatives taste just as nice but can be a lot cheaper.
>
> ❀ If you are providing your own drink but can't get to a warehouse, look out for special offers at your local supermarket. Many do seasonal offers, especially during celebrations such as Christmas, Halloween, Easter and Valentine's Day. If you have some spare storage space, you can always buy all your drink when you see a special offer and store it away ready for the big day.
>
> ❀ If you have to use the venue's catering service, choose foods which are in season and which you won't have to pay extra for.

Real bride's tip

'Look out for special offers throughout the year. Even though we got married in April, we used the festive celebrations to buy our champagne when the offers were on. We even bought our sparklers in November when they had been reduced. It saved us a lot of money – we just had to organise the space to store it all.'

PROVIDING YOUR OWN FOOD AND DRINK

One way to significantly reduce the cost of your food and drink budget is to provide your own. This may not be as daunting as it first sounds. It can actually bring a unique aspect to your wedding, especially if you have themed foods related to your background or if you have a relative famed for a special homemade dish!

There are several menu options for providing your own food, from a simple afternoon tea with sandwiches and cakes to a hot or cold buffet.

AFTERNOON TEA

If you're getting married early in the day, then an afternoon tea is a perfect choice for a meal – at this time of day your guests won't want a heavy meal with lots of food and drink. At an afternoon tea, sandwiches, wraps and cakes are served on tiered dessert platters allowing the guests to help themselves. You can label each sandwich with a small flag and a 'v' to help identify the vegetarian sandwiches. To make the sandwiches more interesting, cut them into small shapes such as hearts, triangles, stars or fingers – this makes it more fun for the guests, especially the children.

It is traditional to serve the afternoon tea with hot non-alcoholic drinks such as tea or coffee, though you can adapt this to whatever you want, whether a glass of champagne or wine, or cold soft drinks such as freshly pressed lemonade or orange juice.

Afternoon tea menu suggestions

Sandwiches or wraps

* Cucumber and cream cheese
* Ham and cheese
* Cheese (brie, cheddar, red Leicester)
* Cheese and pickle
* Cheese and onion
* Beef, mustard and rocket
* Chicken salad
* Pesto chicken
* Chicken tikka
* Prawn salad
* Smoked salmon and cream cheese
* Hummus and roasted peppers
* Avocado, chicken and bacon
* Egg and watercress
* Bacon, lettuce and tomato
* Prawn mayo

- ❀ Mexican bean wrap
- ❀ Crayfish and rocket
- ❀ Roast beef and horseradish
- ❀ Tuna and cucumber

Cakes and desserts

- ❀ Cream fingers
- ❀ Mini doughnuts
- ❀ Scones with jam and cream
- ❀ Brownies
- ❀ Mini-cheesecakes
- ❀ Fairy cakes
- ❀ Fruit tartlets – strawberry, kiwi, blueberry, raspberry
- ❀ Mini muffins
- ❀ Strawberries and cream
- ❀ Mini Victoria sponges
- ❀ Profiteroles

BUFFETS

Having a hot or cold buffet can be a good easy alternative to a sit down meal. It allows the guests more choice over what they want to eat (and how much!). It also allows you to have the food ready on a much more relaxed time schedule.

Buffet menu suggestions

Cold

- ❀ Quiche – bacon and cheese, three cheeses, cheese and onion
- ❀ Cocktail sausages wrapped in bacon
- ❀ Sausage rolls
- ❀ Chicken drumsticks
- ❀ Pork pies
- ❀ Sandwiches

- Cold meat selection – ham, parma ham, pork, beef, chicken, turkey, salami
- Bread
- Olives
- Dips
- Pate
- Pasta salads – tomato, chicken and bacon, pesto, tuna and sweetcorn
- Salads
- Salmon parcels
- Cheese and biscuits
- Couscous
- Roasted vegetables
- Rice salad

Hot

- Soup – vegetable, tomato, mushroom, chicken, onion
- Pasta salads
- Mini burgers
- Pizza
- Hot meats – chicken wings and drum sticks, beef, turkey, lamb, pork
- Quiche and pastry tarts
- Potato skins with cheese and bacon
- Bacon rolls
- Chips
- Nachos
- Chili con carne
- Lasagne
- Garlic bread
- Fish
- Roasted vegetables

HOLDING A BBQ

If you're getting married during the warmer months, a BBQ is the perfect summer option for food. It allows guests to have choice over what they eat and everyone enjoys a good BBQ! If your venue is not supplying the BBQ, you will need to hire the equipment along with a chef (or talented usher) to cook the food.

BBQ menu suggestions

- ❀ Meat – chicken wings, chicken drumsticks, steaks, chops, sausages
- ❀ Burgers – cheese, vegetarian
- ❀ Vegetables – mushrooms, jacket potatoes, corn on the cob, roasted tomatoes
- ❀ Side dishes – coleslaw, potato salad, green salads, pasta salads, rice, couscous
- ❀ Fish – salmon, sea bass, prawns
- ❀ Kebabs
- ❀ Hog roast
- ❀ Stuffed peppers
- ❀ Roasted tomatoes

THEMED FOODS

If you or your groom has connections with another country why not incorporate it into the menu. Or perhaps you'd like to evoke the place you first met, where you got engaged or where you are going on honeymooon – it will be a great talking point at the wedding breakfast.

If you are daunted by the thought of cooking themed food, you could consider hiring people to come in, such as a fish and chip van or an Indian meal supplied by a local restaurant. This will take the pressure off you to get the food prepared beforehand, but could still work out cheaper than a sit-down meal. It will also add an element of fun and surprise to the day. You can also incorporate themed decorations into the wedding breakfast area.

When providing your own food, remember to take into account any allergies your guests may suffer from or if you have any vegetarians or vegans attending. You should ask your guests about any special dietary requests on your invitations so you are prepared well in advance.

CANAPÉS

Canapés are great served with welcome drinks but can be an expensive luxury. If your venue is providing them, you will find that they charge per canapé. If you budget for five to six canapés per person, it can soon add up and on the day you may feel that you don t get value for money.

It is much cheaper to provide your own canapés and place them on a table rather than hire waiters to serve them. This will encourage your guests to eat when they are hungry rather than when they are given food by waiters. You can even have a light finger buffet instead of smaller more expensive canapés.

Making your own canapés doesn't have to be complicated. Here's some inspiration for some easy homemade canapés.

- ❀ Blini – smoked salmon and cream cheese on a cracker/biscuit with a sprig of dill
- ❀ Stuffed tomatoes with cream cheese mixed with herbs
- ❀ Warm toasted bread with cheese and dips
- ❀ Mini quiches
- ❀ Samosas
- ❀ Small cheese scones
- ❀ Mini mozzarella balls on skewers with cherry tomatoes or red peppers
- ❀ Small skewers of chicken with satay sauce
- ❀ Baby plum tomatoes, halved and drizzled with olive oil and basil
- ❀ Small cocktail sausages drizzled with honey
- ❀ Pears wrapped in parma ham and drizzled with lemon juice
- ❀ Vegetarian spring rolls with a chilli dip
- ❀ Mini crab cakes with a lime and chilli mayo
- ❀ Halved figs, griddled and wrapped in prosciutto
- ❀ King prawns with a garlic or chilli dip
- ❀ Sausage or melted cheese rolls

For even easier canapés, check out your local supermarket where you will be able to find party platter canapés, which you can just warm up and serve for even less stress.

WELCOME DRINKS

Serving welcome drinks at the reception venue after the ceremony is a great way to bring everyone together to start mingling and reminiscing about how lovely the ceremony was. You should aim to serve a minimum of two drinks per person to keep the guests busy while you and your new husband have your wedding photographs taken. What you decide to serve as welcome drinks can depend on the season you are getting married in. There are lots of alternatives to serving expensive champagne. Here are some ideas.

Summer wedding

Buck's Fizz, white wine, rose wine, Pimm's, orange and lemonade, alcoholic and non-alcoholic fruit punches, sparkling grape juice, orange juice, fresh lemonade, cocktails such as Mojitos and Cosmopolitans.

Winter wedding

Mulled wine, red wine, hot whisky, alcoholic and non-alcoholic hot fruit punches, hot chocolate (some with a kick of liquor), winter Pimm's, orange juice

Serving suggestions

To make your drinks look more attractive, decorate the glasses with fruit such as strawberries, raspberries or physalis. Simply slice the strawberries in half but not all the way through and gently place them on the rim of the glasses. For an even easier decoration, place raspberries in the bottom of the glasses and pour drinks over the top. This works particularly well with fruit punches and sparkling drinks.

Budget busters

Reduce your drink costs with these simple ideas…

* Cut wine glass costs by serving drinks from large jugs instead of having pre-poured drinks in lots of different glasses. Your guests can keep re-using the same glass unless they have a different drink.
* Look on internet auction sites for cheap glasses to buy. It will make it much more interesting if they are all different and, after all, there's no reason why they all have to match!
* Sparkling cava works just as well as champagne, especially if you decorate the glasses with fresh fruit.
* Make your cava go further by mixing with orange juice to make a refreshing Buck's Fizz.
* Save money on expensive mineral water by providing tap water in jugs. Add ice and lemon to the jugs to make them look more attractive.
* Serving an alcoholic fruit punch will be cheaper than individual cocktails or wine. It will still taste just as nice, but you can bulk out the alcohol with fruit juices, fizzy drinks and pieces of fruit.
* You can double up on your table wine and favours by giving each person a small bottle of wine as their favour, instead of supplying a large bottle of wine per table. You can even personalise the label on the bottle with your initials or your wedding date.
* You can make any cheap drink look more expensive by decorating the glass and adding some colour by pouring a non-alcoholic syrup, fruit puree or fruit juice in the bottom of the glass before adding the main drink (such as a sparkling wine/cava) on top. This will bring a two-tone colour to the drink, making it look much more attractive.
* Get your ushers to pour the welcome drinks instead of having waiters to do it – after all they need to earn their job title!

DESSERTS

One of the best things about a meal is the dessert and a wedding gives you the perfect excuse to indulge. There are many desserts to choose from – so how do you go about selecting one? The easiest option is to provide a dessert trolley, giving your guests the choice of a variety, but this can be expensive. If you are going to provide your own, here's a few simple but really tasty ideas!

- ❀ Raspberry ripple cheesecake – The best thing about cheesecake is that you can alter it to whatever flavour you prefer.
- ❀ Individual chocolate mousse – Chocolate is always a winner and you can add orange, mint or a liquor such as Baileys for a twist.
- ❀ Strawberries and cream – Really easy. You can mix up the strawberries with other fruits such as blueberries or raspberries.
- ❀ Apple crumble and custard – Perfect for cold winter weddings. Try alternatives such as plum or rhubarb if you prefer.
- ❀ Trifle – Layers of tinned fruit, sponge, jelly, custard and cream make this a really easy dessert to make.
- ❀ Ideas for children – Chocolate and orange mousse, jelly and ice cream, fruit and cream, individual mini trifle.

Real bride's tip

'We served our wedding cake as our dessert. It saved us from paying for an extra course and we had been to many weddings where the guests were too full from the wedding breakfast to have any wedding cake. Our wedding cake was so delicious it would have been such a shame if it had been wasted!'

AFTER DINNER DELIGHTS

Truffles served with tea and coffee make a perfect end to a meal. They are so easy to make and can be stored in the fridge up to ten days in advance. The following recipe makes approximately 20 truffles.

Truffles recipe

Ingredients
100ml heavy cream
200g milk chocolate
15g unsalted butter

A few drops of your chosen filling e.g. mint, vanilla, orange extract or liquor, or brandy or cognac for a kick!

Topping
Sifted cocoa powder
Chopped nuts
Grated milk, dark or white chocolate

Tools
Medium-sized bowl
Small saucepan
Plate
Wooden spoon
Foil sweet cases – try to match your wedding colours
Teaspoon

1. Break the chocolate into small pieces in a bowl.
2. Put the cream in a saucepan with the butter and slowly bring to the boil.
3. Pour over the broken chocolate and stir until all the chocolate has melted and you have a smooth consistency.
4. Stir in a few drops of your chosen extract if you are using one.
5. Cover the mixture and allow to cool for about 30 minutes at room temperature. Then transfer the mixture to the fridge and chill for about 2 hours.
6. Using a teaspoon, scoop out bite-sized pieces. Dust your hands lightly with cocoa powder and roll the pieces into balls.
7. Spread your chosen topping onto a plate and roll the truffle balls in it.
8. Place the truffles in individual foil sweet cases and chill.

10

~ *Wedding cakes* ~

When it comes to choosing your wedding cake, there are many options available. From the type of sponge you have to the decorations – the choices are endless. There are also plenty of alternatives to traditional sponge cakes if you prefer something a little different.

TRADITIONAL WEDDING CAKES

Traditional wedding cakes are tiered fruit sponge cakes. However, these days many choose chocolate, lemon or plain sponge as their preference. There are no rules when it comes to choosing the wedding cake – it's completely the preference of the bride and groom, so pick your favourite.

If you're having trouble choosing a flavour and you're thinking of having a tiered sponge, why not split the tiers into different flavours. For example the largest tier could be chocolate, lemon for the middle and fruit for the top tier. This is a good way of pleasing all the fussy eaters!

MAKING A WEDDING CAKE

Making your own wedding cake can save you a lot of money and gives you the opportunity to personalise it to fit with your wedding theme. Here are a few simple wedding cake recipes and, after a few practice runs, making it will be a piece of cake!

'I didn't want to pay out for a wedding cake so I enrolled in a cake-making class. It was lots of fun and I have since made wedding cakes for a few friends, turning it into a money-making hobby.'

Light fruit cake recipe

Fruit cake is the most traditional type of wedding cake. This recipe (see page 99) is for a lighter version than the traditional darker and heavier fruit cake, which makes it perfect to stack as the top tier because of its lighter weight, enabling you to have a larger chocolate bottom tier! This cake will keep up to one month if wrapped well so you can make it well in advance of your wedding day. The recipe serves 24.

Lemon sponge cake recipe

This is a lovely moist sponge with a touch of citrus flavouring (see page 100 for the recipe). You can keep this cake wrapped in baking parchment and cling film for up to four days or freeze it up to a month in advance. This recipe serves 30 people so adjust the quantities to suit your number of guests.

Dark chocolate wedding cake recipe

Everyone loves chocolate and this simple chocolate cake will work a treat with all your wedding guests. This recipe (see page 101) serves 40 people so adjust the quantities to suit your amount of guests. You can make this cake unfilled up to four days in advance or keep it wrapped in baking paper and cling film in the freezer for up to a month. Try filling it with a gorgeous chocolate filling for the ultimate wedding cake!

Light fruit cake recipe

Preparation time: 30mins
Cooking time: 2hrs, 15mins

Ingredients
140g unsalted butter, softened
140g golden caster sugar
2tbsp orange flower water
zest and juice of 1 lemon
zest and juice of 1 orange
175g plain flour
2 large eggs, beaten
100g undyed glacé cherries, halved
100g dried apricots, roughly chopped
50g shelled pistachios, left whole
100g mixed peel, chopped
50g (3 balls) stem ginger from a jar
100g golden sultanas

Tools
15cm round cake tin
Baking or greaseproof paper
Large mixing bowl
Electric whisk
Small bowl
Spoon
Wooden spoon
Metal skewer

1. Preheat the oven to 160°C/Fan 140°C/320°F/Gas Mark 3.
2. Line the bottom of the cake tin with baking paper and lightly grease, along with the sides.
3. Cream the sugar and butter together until light and fluffy, then gradually beat in the eggs a little at a time.
4. In a small bowl, mix the orange flower water with the zest and juice of the orange and lemon.
5. Fold the flour, dried fruit, ginger and pistachios into the creamed mix, then add the zest and juice mix.
6. Spoon the mixture into the tin and bake for 30mins, then turn the oven down to 150°C/ Fan 130°C/300°F/Gas Mark 2 and bake for another 1hr, 45mins. The cake should have risen and be golden. To check if it has cooked right through, insert a skewer and it should come out clean.
7. Leave the cake to cool for 15mins before transferring to a wire rack to cool completely.

Lemon sponge cake recipe

Preparation time: 30mins

Cooking time: 1hr, 15mins

Ingredients
350g golden caster sugar
6 eggs, beaten
350g unsalted butter, softened
280g self-raising flour
140g plain flour
zest of 4 lemons and juice of 3 (about 100ml/3.5 fl oz)

For the syrup:
100g golden caster sugar
zest and juice of 2 lemons

Tools
23cm round cake tin
Baking or greaseproof paper
Large mixing bowl
Electric whisk
Fork
Metal skewer
Saucepan

1. Preheat the oven to 160°C/ Fan140°C/320°F/Gas Mark 3.
2. Line the bottom of the cake tin with baking paper and lightly grease, along with the sides.
3. Cream the sugar and butter together until light and fluffy, then gradually beat in the eggs a little at a time.
4. Fold in both the flours and add a pinch of salt, followed by the lemon zest and juice.
5. Spoon the mixture into the tin and bake for 1hr, 15mins until well risen and golden. You can check if the cake is cooked properly by inserting a skewer and it should come out clean.
6. While the cake is cooking you can start making the syrup. Heat the sugar, lemon zest and juice in a small pan until the sugar dissolves. Set this to one side.
7. When the cake is cooked, leave it to cool until it's just warm. Then using a skewer poke holes all over the sponge right down to the bottom.
8. Pour the syrup over the cake, letting it soak into all the holes. Leave to cool completely before serving or storing. You can use orange zest and juice if you prefer this to lemon.

Dark chocolate wedding cake recipe

Preparation time: 40mins
Cooking time: 2hrs, 30mins

Ingredients
650g plain chocolate
650g unsalted butter
3tsp vanilla essence
100ml strong coffee
650g plain flour
2tsp baking powder
2tsp bicarbonate of soda
10 eggs
950g light soft brown sugar
2 x 284ml soured cream

Tools
30cm round cake tin
Baking or greaseproof paper
Medium-sized saucepan
Sieve
Large mixing bowl
Medium-sized mixing bowl
Wooden spoon
Metal skewer

1. Preheat the oven to 160°C/Fan 140°C/320°F/Gas Mark 4.
2. Line the bottom of the cake tin with baking paper and lightly grease, along with the sides.
3. Put the butter and chocolate into the saucepan and stir over a low heat. Once the chocolate has melted stir in the coffee and vanilla.
4. Sift the flour, bicarbonate of soda and baking powder into a large mixing bowl. Add the sugar.
5. Beat the eggs and soured cream in another bowl and pour into the flour mix.
6. Pour in the melted chocolate mixture and stir well with a wooden spoon.
7. Pour the mixture into the greased tin and cook in the oven for 2hrs, 30 mins. Once cooked, leave the cake in the tin to cool completely.

FILLING YOUR CAKE

A filling can make or break a cake so if you want to fill your wedding cake choose one which compliments the cake's flavour. For example, a chocolate frosting will work well in a chocolate cake, but a vanilla buttercream will probably suit a plain or lemon sponge better.

You can keep the following buttercreams in the fridge for up to a week, but always bring the mixtures back to room temperature and beat well before using. The following recipes make enough to cover a 20cm cake, so adapt them to your requirements. Here are some of the most popular buttercreams for you to try.

Vanilla buttercream

This buttercream works perfectly with a plain or a lightly flavoured sponge such as a lemon cake.

Vanilla buttercream

Ingredients
175g soft butter
300g sifted icing sugar
1tsp vanilla paste or 1 vanilla pod

1. In a bowl beat the butter until light and fluffy.
2. Gradually add the icing sugar one spoonful at a time into the butter mix. Keep beating the mixture until it is pale and creamy.
3. Add the seeds from the vanilla pod or the vanilla paste and beat together.

Chocolate buttercream

This buttercream is perfect for filling or covering a chocolate wedding cake.

Chocolate buttercream

Ingredients
175g butter
125g cocoa powder
650g icing sugar
150ml milk
1tsp vanilla extract

1. In a bowl beat the butter until light and fluffy.
2. Stir in the cocoa and icing sugar alternately with the milk and vanilla extract.
3. Beat the mixture together until it reaches a spreading consistency.

Lemon buttercream

A lemon filling is a perfect choice for a lemon or plain sponge to add some zing!

Lemon buttercream

Ingredients
150g unsalted butter, softened
300g icing sugar
finely grated rind of 1 lemon
splash of milk

1. Beat the butter until light and fluffy.
2. Gradually beat in the icing sugar a little at a time.
3. Mix in the grated lemon rind and beat together. If your mixture is too thick add a splash of milk to reach a spreading consistency.

Real bride's tip

'We cheated when it came to our wedding cake. We used packet sponge mixtures bought from the supermarket and covered them with ready-made frostings. It saved us from making the cake ourselves and stressing over whether it would turn out correctly. Nobody noticed and everyone said our cake was delicious!'

COVERING YOUR CAKE

The easiest way to cover a wedding cake is to use ready-to-roll marzipan, covered with ready-to-roll icing. These are both available from most supermarkets. You can add a touch of food dye to your icing to subtly change its colour to match your colour scheme. Be careful not to use too much food dye though – a couple of drops should be sufficient for pastel colours, otherwise you could end up with a bright pink cake instead of that pale pink colour you wanted! Also be sure to mix it thoroughly for an even result – you don't want to end up with a stripy cake unless that was planned.

ADDING DECORATIONS

For that extra wow factor, add some decoration such as sugar flowers, silver balls, ribbons or even fresh flowers to your wedding cake.

Real bride's tip

'When we were organising our wedding cake, we were shocked by the prices that we were being quoted just for some sponge and icing! We didn't want the extra pressure of making our own cake so we bought three sponge cakes from the supermarket and got a cake maker that we found in the local paper to decorate and construct it for us.'

STACKING YOUR WEDDING CAKE

If you want to create tiers by using pillars on your wedding cake, you should transport each tier separately and assemble the wedding cake at your venue. Never assemble the cake into tiers and then try to transport it – this is just asking for an accident to happen!

The best type of cake for making into tiers is a fruit cake, however it is possible to stack almost any cake. If you're stacking different kinds of cake, make sure you stack the tiers in order of weight with the lightest as the top tier and the heaviest as the bottom. Never try to stack a heavy fruit cake tier on top of a sponge as the weight of the fruit could cause the pillars to sink into the sponge layer. If you want to have fruit cake as the top tier, make a light fruit cake such as the recipe given on page 99.

How to stack a wedding cake

You will need:

A ruler
Pillars (available from wedding shops)
5mm thick dowel

Step-by-step guide to stacking a wedding cake

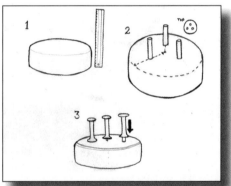

1. Start with the largest bottom tier of the cake. Using a ruler, measure the depth of the cake. Cut 3 to 4 pieces of 5mm dowel (depending on how many pillars you want) to the same depth of the cake plus the height of the pillar.
2. Push each piece of dowel into the cake. The dowel should be positioned halfway between the centre and the edge of the cake.
3. Place each pillar over the piece of dowel and then place the next cake (still on its cake board) on top to create the next tier. If you're having a third tier, you may find it easier to insert the dowel pieces into the second tier before stacking it.

CUPCAKES

Instead of a tiered sponge cake, a popular option with many brides these days is to have a tower of individual cupcakes. This is a good way to introduce several sponge flavours, with either plain or flavoured frostings. The best thing about having a cupcake tower is that every cupcake can be individually personalised to match the guests or your wedding theme. If you still want a cake to cut for photographs, you can have a small sponge as the top tier.

Cupcake recipe

Cup cake recipe

Preparation time: 20mins
Cooking time: 20mins

Ingredients
2 large eggs
1tsp vanilla essence
125g caster sugar
125g soft margarine
125g self-raising flour

Tools
Large bowl
Electric whisk
Cupcake tin
Cupcake cases – try matching these to your wedding colour scheme
Wire rack

1. Preheat the oven to 180°C/Fan 160°C/350°F/Gas Mark 4.
2. Put all the ingredients in a large bowl and using an electric whisk beat them together until the mixture is smooth.
3. Line the cupcake tin with paper cases and half fill each paper case with the cake mixture.
4. Cook the cakes in the oven for 20mins until they have risen and are golden.
5. When cooked, transfer to a wire rack and leave them to cool completely before decorating.

These cupcakes are really easy to make and look delicious when frosted. Choose one of the frostings on pages 102 and 103 to cover your cupcakes and decorate them to match your wedding theme. The following recipe makes enough for 12 people, so adapt it to make enough for all your wedding guests.

There's lots of fun ways to decorate your cupcakes. Here's a few ideas:

- Frostings
- Sweets
- Mini marshmellows
- Dried fruit
- Grated fruit rind
- Nuts
- Sprinkles
- Grated white or dark chocolate
- Silver balls
- Sprinkled icing sugar – you can cut out a cardboard silhouette to create shapes
- Writing icing

ALTERNATIVE OPTIONS FOR WEDDING CAKES

If you're not a fan of sponge cakes, or if you just want something more unique for your wedding cake, there's a number of alternatives.

Biscuit tower

Creating a biscuit tower is a great alternative to sponge cakes and just as much fun! The best thing about biscuit towers is that you can use a variety of different flavours.

From plain to chocolate or nut, you can make your biscuits as plain or extravagant as you want and, for a fun twist, make them into shapes relevant to your wedding theme or personality. This is a simple plain recipe that makes about 30 biscuits.

If you want to vary your biscuits try adding white or dark chocolate chunks, dried fruit or nuts. You can decorate them with coloured icing or even sandwich two together with a filling like a vanilla or chocolate buttercream or a fruit jam to make them even more delicious.

Biscuit tower recipe

Preparation time: 15mins
Cooking time: 15mins

Ingredients
140g caster sugar
250g butter, softened
2tsp vanilla extract
1 egg yolk
300g plain flour

Tools
Large bowl
Electric whisk or fork
Sieve
Shaped cookie cutters – try matching your shapes to your wedding theme
Baking sheet
Wire rack

1. Preheat the oven to 180°C/Fan 160°C/350°F/Gas Mark 4.
2. Mix the butter and sugar in a large bowl.
3. Add the egg yolk and vanilla to the butter mixture and beat well.
4. Sift in the flour and stir until the mixture is well combined. Mix with your hands at the end and press the dough together.
5. Cut out the shapes you want and spread them on a non-stick baking sheet. Remember that the biscuits will expand during cooking so make sure they are not too close together.
6. Bake for 12–15 minutes until they are a pale golden colour, then transfer them to a wire rack and allow them to cool completely before decorating.

Ideas for shapes:

❀ Butterflies
❀ Shoes and bags
❀ Stars
❀ Flowers
❀ Letters
❀ Hearts

The easiest way to display your biscuits is by using a tiered dessert stand. You can find these in most high-street department stores. Use each tier to fan out a selection of biscuits. If you are feeling daring, you can even display some vertically to hide the centre pole of the stand, though you may want to do this at your venue rather than trying to transport it already constructed.

Cheese tower

If you're not a fan of wedding cakes, then simply don't have one. It's your wedding day and if you prefer to have a unique alternative, a cheese tower is a great choice.

Start by deciding on the amount of guests you will need to serve – this will enable you to work out how many layers of cheese you need. Next find out what cheeses your local supermarket or farmers' market supplies in large wheels or blocks. Try and select cheeses with different strengths and colours that come in similar shapes to add some variety to the tower.

To construct the cheese tower, begin by placing the largest wheel of cheese on the bottom. Then depending on how many further tiers of cheese you want, stack each following wheel on top. With each tier the wheel of cheese should gradually get smaller, so that the final, smallest wheel is on the very top for you to cut if you wish for the photographs. Lastly decorate the tower with flowers or fruit such as draping grapes, apricots or apple slices and fan a selection of biscuits and crackers round the base to accompany the cheese.

Budget busters

Save some money on your wedding cake with these top tips.

 If a caterer is making your cake, you will probably be given a quote based on the amount of tiers you have. Stick to as few tiers as possible to reduce the cost.

❀ Try making the wedding cake yourself, or better still ask a talented family member or friend to make it for you. The cake can be your wedding present and they will be honoured to have such an important role.

❀ Buy a cake mixture from a supermarket rather than buying all the ingredients and making the cake from scratch.

❀ Ready-made fillings and marzipan can work out cheaper than buying the individual elements. It will also save a lot of stress as it's guaranteed to taste good!

❀ Look in supermarkets for wedding cakes. It is more common now for them to supply wedding cakes and, if you can't find one to match your exact specifications, buy a plain one from the shelf and decorate it yourself.

❀ Many supermarkets now produce ready-made plain cupcakes, which are great for adding frostings and decorations to. Some even do mini-cupcakes, which are ideal for children.

❀ It's really easy to make your own cheese tower if you're having one. You can buy the cheese directly from a cheese supplier, farm or supermarket and construct the tower yourself.

❀ If you want a three-tiered cake but in fact only have a small number of guests coming so you will in reality only need one tier, have a fake bottom tier. This is more common than you think and once decorated nobody will notice. Just remember to cut the correct tier!

Real bride's tip

'At our wedding we had a grown-up cake for the adults and a tower of small fairy cup-cakes for the children. We iced all the children's names on the cakes and they loved looking for them!'

The wedding dress

After getting engaged, finding your perfect dress will be high on your list of priorities. You will spend many hours researching and trying on dresses, just to find that perfect one – an experience you may find rather overwhelming!

HOW TO FIND YOUR DREAM DRESS

Finding your perfect wedding dress is an experience like no other. You may already have in mind the type of dress you would like, but it's good to try and keep an open mind and not to rule anything out too early. You may start your hunt with one style of dress in mind and end up wearing something completely different on your big day.

Here are some top tips to help you find your dream dress.

❀ Set a budget before you go dress shopping. Avoid looking at dresses over your budget in case you fall in love with one of them – you might not then be able to find another dress that you like as much.

❀ Start a scrapbook before you go dress shopping. Look through magazines and collect cuttings of dresses you like. This will help you build up a picture of the kind of style, colour and theme you like and will help the shop assistant find the styles which match your requirements the closest. Don't just look in wedding magazines – your dream dress may be a cocktail or evening dress.

❀ Try on as many different styles as possible, even if it's one that you thought you had ruled out. This is just to make sure that you definitely don't like a certain style. Dresses in magazines or on clothes racks may look better on your body shape than you'd initially thought, so always double check to avoid any regrets later. Remember you'll only be getting married once so make the most of it!

❀ Don't expect to find your dream dress on your first shopping trip. Finding your perfect dress will be a long process of elimination and something that shouldn't be rushed.

❀ Take along someone honest. What you need when you are trying on dresses is someone who you know will be totally honest with you, such as your best friend or sister. Now is not the time for someone to humour you!

❀ Make an appointment. Always phone the shop ahead of your shopping trip to see if you need to make an appointment – you really don't want to be rushed and bullied into buying something you are not 100% happy with. This is also a good opportunity to check if they stock a particular brand you are interested in and whether they sell accessories such as veils, tiaras and shoes.

❀ Remember that your dress will be fitted to your body shape at a later stage. Do not be disappointed if the dress you are trying on appears to be too big and doesn't fit you properly. Most shops will only carry one large sample size in each style so that as many brides as possible can try it on. When you order your dress you will probably order it to the nearest dress size and then it will be altered and fitted at a later stage to fit your body shape precisely.

❀ Decide on your underwear and shoes. When you go for your alterations, make sure you take along the underwear and shoes you are planning to wear on your wedding day. These will both have an impact on the shape and length of your dress, so make sure you have these already decided and bought beforehand.

DECIDING ON A DRESS SHAPE FOR YOUR FIGURE

As you begin to look around for a wedding dress, you will discover that there are many different types of dress shapes available. Each type suits a different body shape, so here's a quick guide to help you decide on the dress style for you.

Princess

One of the most popular styles of wedding dress, this type of gown looks great on all shapes and sizes and many brides choose it for the 'fairytale' effect!

A-line

This shape of gown can be extremely flattering on both small or large-busted brides and suits most figures whether tall or short.

Two piece dresses

A two piece gown is good for brides who may not necessarily have an upper torso in proportion to their bottom half. The great advantage of this type of style is that you can buy it in two separate sizes and tailor it to fit your figure without having to squeeze into something too small (or large), which may make you feel uncomfortable on your big day.

Fishtail

A wonderful choice for curvy figures with small waists and big hips and bottoms.

Straight cut

This type of gown suits a range of figures. It particularly flatters straight, tall figures with small busts and hips.

Real bride's tip

'Even though I wanted a strapless dress, I felt self-conscious about my upper arms so I bought a lace bolero from the high street. I didn't end up wearing it after all as I felt beautiful enough in my dress but it made me feel better knowing it was there if I wanted it.'

Real bride's tip

'I chose my dress from one I had seen and tried on in an expensive wedding shop. Unfortunately it was way out of my budget, so I got a similar one made overseas at a fraction of the cost. I supplied a picture of the dress I wanted and had to order it way in advance of my wedding day. When it arrived I was really happy with it. The measurements were a little big so I had to get some adjustments made and the fabrics weren't as luxurious as the original dress, but the amount of money I saved was definitely worth it. Everyone commented on how beautiful the dress was and I put the money I had saved towards some designer shoes I had always wanted!'

CHOOSING THE RIGHT FABRIC

When picking your gown, keep in mind that it may come in a range of different colours and fabrics. Your wedding shop will probably have fabric swatches to show you all the possible choices. The fabric you choose should be carefully considered, especially if you're getting married in a hot climate. Choose a light fabric for hot destinations and for ease of transport. Remember, when you try on a dress in the shop it will be for no longer than 30 minutes, but on the big day it will be for several hours.

Here's a selection of fabrics for you to consider for your dress.

Chiffon

This is a very light fabric, which is used mainly as a top layer or for sleeves and necklines.

Duchess satin

Completely the opposite from chiffon, duchess satin is one of the heaviest fabrics. While it is very beautiful to look at and touch, it should be avoided for weddings in hot climates because of its weight.

Silk georgette

Like chiffon, this is a light fabric usually used as a top layer. It is a gorgeous fabric to touch and has a lovely floaty texture to it.

Lace

Sometimes lace can look a little tacky when used in dressmaking, however when it is used in the right way it can be a beautiful fabric to have on your wedding gown. Lace looks best used as a top layer, as sleeves or on necklines in small, delicate areas.

Budget busters

Get your dream dress and save some money by using these brilliant top tips.

❀ Don't just look in wedding shops for your dress. Many high street shops are now selling good quality wedding dresses at a fraction of the cost of those in wedding shops.

❀ Don't rule out buying a second-hand dress. Scour your local paper or look on eBay for wedding dresses. The chances are that they've only been worn a handful of times, then packed away. And you can usually guarantee that they have been very well looked after!

❀ Most wedding shops will have an end of season clearance sale, where they sell off their in-house sample dresses. This is a great place to pick up a bargain dress. Don't be put off by the size of the dress as you can always get it altered to fit your figure later.

❀ If you see a dress you like in a shop, approach a dressmaker to see if they can replicate it for a fraction of the cost. Most dress shops won't let you take a photo of the dress until you have paid a deposit, so take along a pad and pencil to sketch it as soon as you've left the shop. Alternatively, try to find out who the designer is and see if you can find a picture on the internet.

❀ Unless you are buying one off the peg, most wedding dresses take approximately 12 to 14 weeks to be made. Make sure you leave at least 8 weeks on top of this to allow you time to try on dresses and make your decision. If you need your dress sooner, you will probably be charged a higher fee to rush it through.

❀ The more alterations you need to have made to your wedding dress, the more money you will be charged, so avoid any drastic crash diets or changes in measurements to keep these alterations (and costs) to a minimum.

❀ If you are buying your dress, veil and tiara in the same shop, try to negotiate a discount.

THE VEIL

Traditionally the bride wore a veil to hide her face from the groom until the last moment as a form of modesty. Today many brides still wear veils but to accessorise their dress and hairstyle, rather than to hide their face.

Veils come in many different lengths and in a number of tiers. Here are some of the most popular lengths and styles.

54 inch veil

This veil is a good length for brides who want to create some height and impact. It reaches to the shoulders and can come in a number of tiers to create volume.

72 inch veil

This is one of the most popular lengths of veils as it reaches the waist and creates movement. It can come in a number of tiers and is good for brides of all heights.

108 inch veil

This length reaches to the floor and creates a beautiful, traditional look. Most veils at this length have three tiers – the first ends at the shoulders, the second at the waist and the third at the floor.

126 and 144 inch veils

The longest lengths possible, these veils add a 'wow' factor to any wedding dress. If your dress has little detail on the back then this length is the perfect choice for you – just keep in mind that you may want to remove it later for dancing!

> ## Real bride's tip
>
> 'While I didn't want to wear a second-hand dress on my wedding day, I didn't mind buying a second-hand veil. I found one online and added some lace trimming to the bottom to match the detail on my dress.'

> ## Real bride's tip
>
> 'I found the veil to be a very expensive area and I wasn't prepared to pay hundreds of pounds out for a thin piece of material, so I made my own. I researched on the internet for a pattern and bought some material from a local fabric shop, along with a grip to attach the veil to. On the day itself you would never of known that it was homemade.'

CHOOSING YOUR BRIDESMAID AND FLOWER GIRL DRESSES

Once you have ordered your wedding dress, or at least have an idea of what you want, choosing your bridesmaid and flower girl dresses will next be on your list of things to do.

It will make your decisions easier if you have already chosen a colour scheme or theme for your wedding day. Remember that your bridesmaids are there to compliment you and not the other way around, so think carefully before deciding too quickly. But where do you start? Here are some things to keep in mind when choosing the dresses.

❀ What season are you getting married in? Certain colours look better in different seasons, for example light coloured fabrics such as baby blue and pink work well for summer dresses, while deeper colours such as dark red and plum are well suited to the winter months.

❀ Do you want your bridesmaids to wear long or short dresses?

❀ Do you mind if your bridesmaids have slightly different details to their dresses? For example, older bridesmaids may prefer strapless dresses whereas younger bridesmaids may like dresses with straps.

❀ While it is your wedding day and you have the final say over any decisions, you want your bridesmaids to feel comfortable in what they are wearing. Try to take into consideration any body issues your bridesmaids may have before you go dress shopping. You can ask them to give you a short list with styles they particularly loathe (or love!).

❀ As well as supplying dresses for your wedding day, you may be thinking about buying your bridesmaids shoes too. Before buying the shoes think about their heights, especially if you have any tall bridesmaids who may over shadow you.

❀ If you are having a younger flower girl, try not to buy her dress too early. Young girls can grow and change a lot in a short period of time, so you don't want to order her dress too early and discover she doesn't fit into it by the time your wedding day arrives.

Budget busters

As well as saving money on your wedding dress, it is also possible to save some pennies on your bridesmaids' outfits by following these simple tips.

❀ Look in high street shops for elegant dresses instead of buying actual bridesmaid dresses from wedding shops. If you are worried that one of your guests may wear the same dress to your wedding, accessorise the dresses by adding beads and ribbon to make them look different.

❀ Ask your bridesmaids to buy their own shoes, or perhaps they could wear a pair they already own (especially if the dresses are long and their feet may not be seen anyway).

❀ Most bridesmaid ranges also have dresses in a similar style for the flower girl. However, look in department stores for pretty party dresses as these will be a fraction of the cost and it will be more likely that she can wear the dress again afterwards.

❀ Encourage your bridesmaids not to go on any crash diets between the time you order the dresses and the time they arrive. Like your gown, your bridesmaids' dresses will be ordered at a standard dress size then altered to fit their body shapes. The more alterations they need, the more money it will cost you.

Hair and make up

Every bride wants to look her best on her wedding day and choosing the right hairstyle and make up is a major factor in achieving this. But while there are many make up artists and hairdressers available for you to hire, with just a little inspiration and a bit of practice you too can achieve Hollywood glamour without the Beverly Hills' price tag!

STARTING A BEAUTY REGIME

To get glowing skin and silky hair for the wedding day, every bride should start a beauty regime about six months before the big day. Just a few minutes a week will help to make you feel fabulous on the day. A beauty regime isn't about losing weight, it's about looking after your body so you have perfect skin and glossy hair, which will make you feel and look utterly fabulous.

It would be great if you could afford expensive creams, hair products and facials once a week, but starting a regime doesn't have to mean expensive visits to beauty salons as there's plenty of ways to look after your body and the pennies in your pocket.

A SIMPLE BEAUTY REGIME TO FOLLOW

Exfoliate once a week

Exfoliation gets rid of dry, flaky and dead skin, allowing your skin to become silky, smooth and radiant. It's also a really good thing to do before applying fake tan as it helps even out the colour.

Use a body brush or exfoliating gloves and scrub in gentle, circular motions. An exfoliating cleanser is an alternative to using a brush or pair of gloves. Make sure your body is always wet when you apply the cleanser and be especially careful on delicate areas such as your neck and face. Don't forget to apply it to other less interesting areas, which may also be on display such as your elbows and feet. Always apply a moisturiser after exfoliating as your skin can dry out.

Drink plenty of water

This may seem like the most obvious advice, but don't under-estimate the effect that drinking plenty of water can have on your skin. You should aim to drink at least ten glasses of water a day to hydrate your skin and help flush out toxins from your body. If you find drinking water boring try adding a slice of lemon or orange or a sprig of mint.

Moisturise

Moisturise your skin daily, especially after a bath or shower when soap can dry it out. Remember to moisturise the parts of your body which will be on display the most such as your face, neck, back, feet and hands for those all important ring shots!

Lips

Get luscious lips for your big day by brushing weekly with a dry toothbrush. This will remove dead flaky areas, leaving behind soft kissable lips. If you suffer through the winter months with chapped lips, always carry around a pot of Vaseline or lip seal to apply in an emergency.

Teeth

With the amount of photographs you'll have taken, great teeth are a must! Brush your teeth twice a day and floss at least once a day.

Avoid staining your teeth through drinking fruit juices and fizzy drinks by drinking through a straw. If you do drink lots of fizzy drinks, try to drink a glass of water straight after which will help to clean your enamel. If you want to get your teeth whitened especially for your big day there's lots of home products available from the high street which are nearly as good as the dentist treatments and a lot kinder on your purse. Just make sure that you do any treatments at least four to six weeks before your wedding day in case there are any complications.

Caffeine

As part of your beauty regime, avoid drinking caffeine or at least try and cut down. Caffeine not only stains your teeth, it also contains toxins that can dry out your skin.

Hair

Keep your hair in great condition with regular visits to the salon (or to a friend who you trust with a pair of scissors) in the months leading up to your wedding. Having your hair trimmed every six weeks will stop you from getting dry split ends. A weekly or fortnightly hair conditioning treatment will also improve its appearance and strength. These treatments are available in high street shops for a fraction of the cost of a salon treatment.

If you are thinking about having a drastic hairstyle change, wait until after the wedding. Any chance of having your wedding day ruined by a bad hair decision should be avoided at all costs!

Feet

Don't neglect your feet from your beauty regime, especially if you are wearing a pair of pretty open-toed sandals where they will be on display. Exfoliate once a week to get rid of hard, dry skin, especially around your big toes and heels. Try to moisturise your feet daily and especially after exfoliating and keep your toenails trimmed to avoid brittle nails. It's always good to paint your nails with a clear varnish, which will help them stay strong and avoid splitting.

Nails

Keep your nails in tip-top condition for that all-important ring shot by trimming and shaping at least once a week. This will strengthen the nails and prevent them from becoming brittle and snapping. Try to keep them strong by applying a clear varnish, especially if you regularly catch them during your daily life. When you moisturise your hands, remember to moisturise around the nails as well.

Massage

A great way to relax after all the weeks of stress leading up to the big day is to have a weekly massage. You don't need to go to a beauty salon – why not ask your future husband to give you a massage and vice-versa? It will be great chilling-out time for the pair of you and something you can easily do while relaxing in front of the television.

BEAUTY TREATMENTS

Having beauty treatments such as facials, face masks or a face scrub will help your skin glow on your big day. You should start any facial treatments at least a couple of months before your wedding day so that your skin can get used to the treatment. Don't worry if you come out in spots at first as this is a good sign that your skin is trying to flush out toxins. Also it's better that this happens in the months leading up to the wedding rather than on the wedding day itself!

HOMEMADE BEAUTY TREATMENTS

Homemade beauty treatments are great. Not only are they cheap and easy to make, but they also use up products found in your kitchen cupboard. Here are a few of the best ones for you to make part of your beauty regime.

Honey facemask

> 1tbsp honey
> 1tsp olive oil
> 1 egg yolk

Beat the egg yolk with the oil and then blend in the honey. Apply the mixture to your face and leave on for 15mins, before rinsing off with warm water.

Avocado facemask

> ½ ripe avocado
> Splash of olive oil

Mash the avocado in a bowl and add a splash of olive oil to make the consistency smoother. Apply the mixture to your face and let it set for about 20mins. Wash off with warm water.

Banana facemask

> ½ banana
> 1tbsp honey
> 2tbsp sour cream

Mash the banana in a bowl and add the honey and sour cream. Apply the mixture to your face and leave to set for 10mins. Wash off with a damp cloth.

Pineapple facemask

> 4 large pineapple chunks (these can be from a can)
> 3tbsp olive oil

In a blender combine the pineapple chunks and olive oil until almost smooth. Apply the mixture to your face and leave to set for about 15mins. Wash off with a damp cloth.

Honey and sea salt face scrub

4tbsp sea salt
2tbsp honey

Grind the salt a little so the pieces are not too large. Mix the honey with the salt and gently apply to your face in small circular motions. Wash off with a damp cloth.

Oat and honey face scrub

1tbsp porridge oats
1tbsp honey
Squeeze of lemon juice
Splash of warm water

Mix all the ingredients in a small bowl and add a splash of warm water to thin the mixture to a spreading consistency. Gently apply to your face in small circular motions. Wash off with a damp cloth.

WEDDING HAIR

Once you've decided on a dress, your next big decision will be what to do with your hair. You want to pick a hairstyle that will compliment the rest of your wedding styling and make you look stunning!

There are many ways to have your hair on your wedding day – up, down, curly or straight, the choices are endless. Your hairstyle is a very important choice not only for the day itself but for every time you reflect back on your photographs, so it has to be one that you are comfortable with. But before you make your decision here's a few things you may want to consider.

❀ On your wedding day, do you want to look like yourself or do you want to look completely different?

❀ Does your dress have any important details such as a back detail, which you wouldn't want to cover up?

❀ Does your dress or wedding evoke a period era or theme that you would like to match your hair to?

❀ Are you getting married in a hot climate where an up-do may be better for the heat?

❀ What jewellery will you be wearing? If you have a necklace or pair of earrings that you would like to wear, would it be easier to see them with an up-do?

❀ How are your bridesmaids having their hair? Perhaps you would like to match their hairstyles to yours or have them completely different?

Gather some ideas

Once you have some sense of what you want, research ideas on the internet and magazines and make a scrapbook of looks you like. If anything, this process could give you a clear indication of what you don't want!

LONG HAIR

There are many more style options with longer than shorter hair. You have the advantage of being able to have your hair in an up-do or have it down.

Choosing an up-do

The most important factor when choosing an up-do is to choose a style that will suit your face shape. Round face shapes suit high up-dos and sleek styles, while long-shaped faces suit styles with volume and width. People with oval and heart-shaped faces are lucky as they suit just about any style.

Chignon

How to tie a chignon

A chignon is perfect for a chic, romantic look for both day and night. This is a really easy style to perfect and you can add a twist to it by wearing it on the side or adding some flowers or sparkly clips.

1. Tie your hair in a low ponytail, either in the centre or to the side.
2. Wind your ponytail in your hand to create a twisted effect.
3. Keeping your hair twisted, wrap it around a hair band then fix in place with a grip.

For extra detail, pull a few strands of hair loose and either curl or keep straight.

Twisted up-do

An alternative to a chignon is a twisted up-do – perfect for wearing with a tiara.

1. Gather your hair back into a mid-high ponytail.
2. Without securing in a hair band, twist the hair in your hand.
3. Keeping your hair twisted, pull the hair upwards towards your crown.
4. Twist your hair round and secure with a grip. The ends of the hair should end up on top of your head. Back comb the tuff of hair left on top of your head, then add a tiara in front of your hair and secure in place with a grip if necessary.

How to tie a twisted up-do

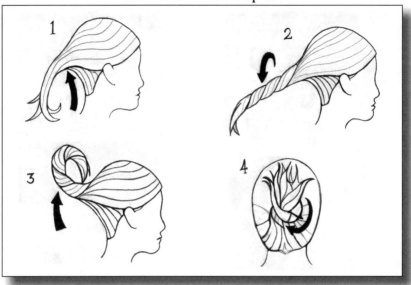

Loose ponytail

Although this style sounds quite casual, a loose ponytail can be an elegant relaxed wedding style. You can wear your ponytail at the back or on the side. Don't leave this style bare, add flowers or sparkly clips to make it dressier or even curl the loose hair in the ponytail.

Simple styles

You don't have to have an up-do on your wedding day to look special. Many brides opt to have a more casual style where they feel more like themselves.

Clipped back

A popular wedding style is to wear half your hair down and half up. This is a really easy hairstyle to get right and is perfect for brides who want to sweep their hair away from their face but still have the feel of a casual hairstyle.

1. Gather the front sections of hair from each side.

2. Pin both sides of your hair together at the back of the head. For an even more casual style, you can plait these sections of hair together. You can add volume to this look by back combing the top section of hair to heighten this area or by adding curls.

How to wear your hair clipped back

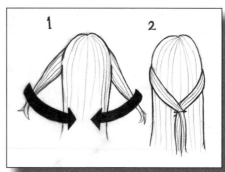

Curled hair

Whether you opt for tight curls or a simple tousled look, curls can add a romantic look to any dress. Create curls by using curling tongs or, for deeper set curls, use rollers on wet hair and set with hairspray. After you have removed the rollers run a wide toothed comb through the hair and allow them to 'drop' as much as required. This hairstyle is very easy to achieve, especially if you have a bridesmaid or friend to help.

Side styles

Sweeping sides can add a romantic feel to hair being left down. It is a perfect option for when you're not sure whether you want your hair up or down.

How to wear your hair in a side style

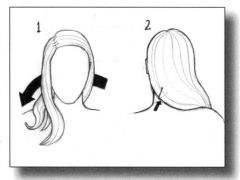

1. Sweep your hair to one side of the nape of your neck.

2. Secure the hair in place with a discreet clip at the back of the hair, which allows the hair to fall over the shoulder

Try adding a fresh flower or sparkly clip to complement the style.

Finishing touches

Try finishing off your hairstyle with some clips, jewels or flowers. These accessories can add some extra sparkle and colour and can tie in with your wedding day colour scheme. Clips with gems on them can add a stunning sparkling effect (especially in photographs), while small flowers and jewels can be scattered among curls or wired into an up-do.

SHORT HAIR

Don't be worried that if you have short hair it will look boring on your wedding day – there's still ways to 'dress' your hair to make it look more special for your big day.

Flowers

Flowers are perfect for adding to short hair. Pin a couple of fresh flower heads into one side of your hair for an elegant look.

Hair band or tiara

Add a bit of sparkle to your hair with a hair band or tiara. Backcomb the back section of your hair to add volume and place the hair band or tiara in front.

Clips

If you don't feel comfortable wearing a hair band or tiara, use some clips instead. Slide a couple of sparkly clips either side of your head for a simple look.

PRACTICE MAKES PERFECT

Whether you are having a complicated up-do or a more casual down style, make sure you practise before the big day. Not only will this give you a chance to perfect the look, but it will also allow you to work out what is the best condition for your hair to be in on the day. For example, if you are having a sleek up-do it may be better to wash your hair the day before and not on the day itself, so it's not too clean and won't fall out of place easily.

When it comes to having your hair styled on the day, make sure you wear a button-up shirt or dressing gown so you don't ruin the hairstyle by taking your top off over your hair.

CHOOSING THE PERFECT HAIR ACCESSORIES

Veils

It is important to consider your veil when choosing your hairstyle. Veils should compliment your hairstyle, not hide it. It's best to choose your veil after deciding on your hairstyle – you can then select the correct length for your wedding day look.

Veils come in many lengths from short shoulder styles to long floor lengths and in different amounts of tiers. Some veils look better sat at the back of the head under an up-do, while others look nicer sat on top of the crown. It is important to try out your veil with your hairstyle to see which you prefer.

Fascinators

A good alternative to a veil is to wear a fascinator. A fascinator is a hair accessory, often on a comb or headband. They are easy and comfortable to wear and can have a number of accessories attached to them to compliment your dress such as feathers, netting, beading or crystals. They are often small and delicate but you can wear one as large and extravagant as you like!

Hats

If you don't feel comfortable wearing a veil or fascinator on your wedding day then a hat is a good solution. Different people suit different styles of hats, so find the right one for you. Tall people can wear most styles of hats while shorter people should wear hats with an upward brim to help draw the eye upwards and help make you look taller.

Tiaras

It's not surprising that tiaras are still the most popular hair accessory for brides, as they add that perfect finishing touch and make you feel like a real princess on your big day!

There are many different types of tiaras to choose from and you should only choose your tiara once you have decided on your dress. Try and match the detail on the tiara to the detail on your dress – for example, if you have crystals on your dress try to find a tiara with small crystals on it rather than pearls.

The size of your tiara is also important. If you have a small head don't choose a tiara that is too tall otherwise it will overpower the impact of your dress. Also, if you want to have a hairstyle with lots of volume think about where the tiara will sit so it is not hidden.

Don't feel shy about trying on as many tiaras as you wish, but remember to try them on with your veil as well to make sure the length and style of your veil compliments your choice of tiara.

Flowers

Many brides these days choose to wear real flowers in their hair instead of veils, tiaras or fascinators. Flowers create a romantic, relaxed look and are perfect for casual weddings or weddings abroad where it is too hot to wear a veil.

There are several different ways to wear real flowers. The most common is to wear one or two large flower heads either on the side of your head or around your up-do, secured in place with small clips. Alternatively you can attach a couple to a hair grip with a short piece of cotton thread and place in your hair. If you want something that looks a little different, you can thread several small flower heads onto a short piece of wire and thread through or around your up-do or wear them on a headband. If you are having a flower girl she might like to wear a headband with small flowers threaded onto it.

WEDDING MAKE UP

You want to look your best on your special day so make sure you plan your make up carefully well in advance. Your make up should complement your dress and hairstyle and not over dramatise the style of the wedding.

Whether you are doing your make up yourself or getting a friend to do it you should remember the following.

- ❀ Your make up should be an enhancement of what you would normally wear. Your wedding day isn't the right time to be trying out a new dramatic look. Remember that your fiancé is marrying you for you, so you want him to recognise you when you walk down the aisle.
- ❀ You should feel comfortable in the make up you are going to wear. If you don't usually wear make up or normally wear just a little, stick to neutral colours.
- ❀ If you are supplying the make up yourself, invest in a few key, good quality pieces such as a good waterproof mascara and lipstick. You want your make up to last all day and cheap stuff will quickly fall off after all the hugs and kisses you will receive!
- ❀ Take into account the season you are getting married in when planning your make up. Avoid anything too shiny on your face in the summer, as this will make you look like you are sweating in photographs. Winter make up can be more dramatic, although it's best to stick to a stronger version of your usual make up than trying anything too over-the-top.

MAKE UP MUST HAVES FOR BRIDES

Ensure you look your best on your wedding day by having these key tools close to hand.

Concealer

Choose a concealer which matches your skin tone and foundation exactly. Most brides will have a concealer they are used to using in their everyday lives so stick to what you know. A concealer which is too light will flag up any imperfections rather than hide them and the same is true with a concealer which is too dark.

Foundation

Prepare your skin by wearing a foundation base. Not only will it make your skin appear smooth, it will help keep the rest of your make up in place too.

Waterproof mascara

Mascara is essential as it opens up the eyes and investing in waterproof mascara is crucial for those emotional moments. To make your eyes look bigger and whiter choose a dark navy mascara. If you are dark skinned or have brown eyes, then black is usually best. Brown mascara can make your eyes look tired.

Blusher or bronzer

For a subtle glow, add some colour to your cheeks with either a pink blusher or bronzer. Apply the colour to the apples of your cheeks, however don't go too harsh especially if you are drinking which can give you a natural flush without the blush.

Eyelash curlers

Curling your eyelashes before applying mascara will make your eyelashes appear longer and make your eyes look more defined in photographs.

Lip pencil and lipstick

To make your lipstick last all day, base your lips with a lip liner before applying your lipstick. This will help keep your lipstick in place. Avoid wearing lip-gloss as it will quickly come off.

Perfume

Investing in a perfume for your special day is a must. Every time you wear it in the future you will be reminded of your special day and the wonderful memories that go with it.

> *Real bride's tip*
>
> *'I got my fiancé to pick out a perfume for me to wear on my wedding day and didn't find out which one it was until the actual day. It was a lovely surprise to think he had picked that one out and I wear it on all our special occasions.'*

TOOLS OF THE TRADE

To be able to apply your make up correctly on the big day, make sure you have the following pieces of equipment to hand.

❀ Large headband – In case you apply your make up before doing your hair.

❀ Cotton buds – To wipe away any smudges.

❀ Sponge – For applying a foundation base.

✿ Two big blusher brushes – One for foundation powder and one for applying blusher or bronzer.

✿ Eyelash curlers – To make your lashes appear as big as possible.

✿ Two small brushes – One for concealer and another for lipstick.

✿ Nail varnish remover – To remove any old fingernail or toenail varnish.

A STEP-BY-STEP GUIDE TO DOING YOUR OWN WEDDING DAY MAKE UP

Look and feel beautiful on your special day by following this simple step-by-step guide.

Moisturise

Moisturise your skin, including face, neck, chest and arms, especially if you have just got out of the bath or shower where your skin may have dried out by using soap products.

Concealer and foundation

The first step for doing your make up is to create a base using foundation. Apply the foundation to your entire face with a brush or sponge. Then use a concealer to cover any blemishes.

If you have perfect skin you may be tempted to skip the foundation base, however you should always use a base as this helps keep the rest of your make up in place for the entire day.

Blusher

Created in gel, liquid and powder form, blusher will give you a lovely glow on your wedding day. Apply the colour to the apples of your cheeks and gradually brush the colour upwards and downwards until it is fully blended. If you are unsure where the apples of your cheeks are, smile when applying the blusher and your apples are the highest point on your cheeks.

If you don't usually use blusher, only use a small amount so you don't look like a clown on your wedding day!

Lips

Start by lining your lips with a colour similar to the one you've chosen for your lipstick so it's not too obvious. Line all around your lips, focusing especially on the bow of your mouth and below your lower lip. Next using a lip brush, fill in your lips with your chosen lipstick. Blot your lips onto a piece of tissue paper so you get rid of any loose colour on the tissue rather than on your groom!

Eye make up

To ensure your eye make up stays in place all day, base your eyes first with a dot of foundation. Next start applying the eye colour from the crease of your eye outwards. It works well to use at least two different tones of the same hue, with the darkest applied to the inside of the eye graduating to the lightest towards the brow. Darker coloured eyes usually suit plum or rosy coloured shades, while lighter coloured eyes such as green or blue look nice with shades of pink and brown. But do experiment in advance to find out which colours you prefer.

After applying eye shadow you need to apply eyeliner and mascara. Decide whether you want to use a pencil liner or a liquid liner for a more dramatic effect. Many people find liquid eyeliners a little tricky to use as you need a steady hand, so if you think you may be a bit wobbly on your wedding day stick to the pencil liner. Run the liner along the rim of your top eyelid and then draw a line on your lower eyelid. To finish your eyes, sweep some mascara on your top lashes.

Finish your make up with a spritz of perfume to smell as gorgeous as you look!

For the best results you should have at least two make up trial runs before the big day, even if you are doing it yourself, to give you a chance to experiment with colours and style.

Bridesmaids' make up

When planning your make up for your wedding, don't forget to think about the bridesmaids' look too. They should have an understated version of your make up, using similar colours and tones.

If you are letting the bridesmaids do their own make up, don't feel shy about giving them a few guidelines. You don't want them turning up wearing clashing eye shadows or with a style which overpowers your look, so talk your ideas through with them beforehand. You could even have a fun evening where all the bridesmaids come round and discuss and try out make up looks for your wedding.

WEDDING DAY EMERGENCIES

No bride wants to think about anything going wrong on her big day, but it's always best to be prepared for the worst. Here's a few emergency remedies should you need them.

Sunburn

If you're getting married abroad, you may be tempted to relax in the sun in the days before the wedding. Try and avoid sunbathing in direct sunlight as you may get uneven tan marks or sunburnt. If the worse does happen and you do get sunburnt, apply aloe vera or vitamin E cream immediately to the affected areas and avoid any more contact with the sun. If your face has turned quite red, you can use a green-toned correcting foundation, which will help balance the redness, but blend it in well so you don't look like an alien!

Flushed skin and rashes

If you break out in rashes under stress or nerves, apply lotion to help soothe the skin. Take time out to relax and calm down and if all else fails try and cover the affected areas with concealer and foundation. Once the day starts your nerves will calm down and so will the rash.

Puffy eyes

It's quite common for brides-to-be to not get much sleep the night before their wedding, which can result in puffy eyes on the wedding morning. If this happens, splash some ice cold water on your face and lie down for 20 minutes with cold tea bags, cucumber slices or a cold flannel over your eyes. This should stop the puffiness – then let the wonder of make up do the rest!

Spots

If typically you come out in a spot on the day of your wedding, try not to panic! Squeeze the spot to drain the fluid as early as possible then apply an ice cube to calm the redness. Later moisturise the area, then apply a concealer and translucent powder to hide the shininess. Once you have all your make up on, your hair styled and you are looking gorgeous in your dress, nobody will notice that spot, I promise!

Touching up make up throughout the day

It's not surprising that with all the hugging, kissing, eating and drinking you'll do throughout the day, you may need to touch up your make up at least once before the day ends.

Instead of carrying round your entire make up bag, you just need a few key pieces which you can ask your chief bridesmaid to carry in her handbag:

- ❀ Small mirror – To quickly check your make up.
- ❀ Translucent powder – For touch ups and to keep shine to a minimum.
- ❀ Lipstick – Keep your lips looking luscious.
- ❀ Mascara – Add instant wow to tired looking eyes.

And a couple of things that aren't make up, but could still prove invaluable on the day:

- ❀ Safety pins – A couple of small safety pins can come in useful for many things especially if there's any wedding dress disasters.
- ❀ Plasters – Your wedding shoes may look beautiful, but your feet may not agree after a few hours.
- ❀ Perfume – To keep you smelling gorgeous.

If there's enough room in your bridesmaids' bag, investing in a pair of fold-up ballet shoes could be a good move. Towards the end of the night, most brides just want to throw off their shoes and dance the night away.

Real bride's tip

'One of my favourite memories of the day is dancing with all my friends at the end of the evening. But my feet were killing me and I wished I had bought along a pair of flat shoes to change into.'

Budget busters

Use these top tips to look good and still save some cash…

❀ Asking a friend to trim your hair regularly instead of visiting a salon will save you lots of money and valuable time.

❀ Buying home conditioning treatments and doing them yourself will be far cheaper than having a professional treatment done. You only need to do them fortnightly to help you achieve that silky glow.

❀ Ask a friend or relative to do your wedding hair instead of hiring a professional. It will work out a lot cheaper and there's no reason why it won't look just as nice!

❀ Ask your bridesmaids to do their own hair instead of hiring a hairdresser to do it for them. They could even do each other's to save some time.

❀ If there's a particular perfume you would like to wear on your wedding day, see if you know anyone who could lend it to you for the day to save you from buying it.

❀ If you have a friend who always has stunning make up, ask her for some free lessons and tips for your own wedding day make up.

❀ Buying make up brushes can be expensive. See if you can borrow some from friends or relatives. Just remember to wash the brushes in warm water before and after you've used them to stop any germs spreading.

❀ Hit the seasonal sales to buy the make up you need for your wedding day. Remember to put it away somewhere safe so you don't get tempted to use it before hand.

❀ Sales are also a great time for buying any expensive creams, face treatments or perfumes you wouldn't normally be able to afford.

Real bride's tip

'Don't be afraid to ask fellow brides to borrow a tiara or veil. My best friend got married six months before I did and we decided to share the cost of some things like the tiara and veil. This halved the costs and it was nice to know that they got used more than once.'

Favours

Wedding favours are traditionally given to each guest at the wedding breakfast. They are an old tradition that originated in Italy, where five sugared almonds were given as a gift to each guest. The five sugared almonds symbolise wealth, health, fertility, long life and happiness. These days, favours can be anything from a simple chocolate to bath salts. Some people even choose to donate money to charity instead of giving out favours.

Favours are not compulsory and choosing not to give your guests any will save you money. Your guests will not think any less of you and I have been to many weddings where the favours are still left on the table at the end of the night, so think carefully before spending money on them – will it really make a difference to your wedding if you choose not to give them?

IDEAS FOR FAVOURS

If you do want to give your guests favours, here are some cheap and unique ideas.

- ❀ A single chocolate – Present this by itself either wrapped in some tissue paper or in a small box.
- ❀ Candles
- ❀ Bar of natural soap
- ❀ Potpourri

❀ Seeds – Ask your guests to plant a flower or vegetable or fruit plant in memory of your wedding day. You can present the seeds in a small envelope or wrapped in tissue paper with a small instruction card. The flower could be one from your wedding bouquet or just your favourite fruit or vegetable.

❀ Charity donation – The average favour costs £1 per guest. If there's a charity close to your heart, why not donate the money to it instead of buying favours. You can leave cards on the table telling your guests which charity you have donated to on their behalf.

❀ Lottery scratch cards – A fun alternative to traditional favours and, who knows, a guest may leave your wedding a lot richer!

❀ Raffle tickets – A cheaper alternative to scratch cards, but just as much fun. Leave a raffle ticket for each guest on the dinner table (either in a small envelope or perhaps pinned to the centrepiece) and then call out numbers for the raffle. You have more control over the prizes and, unlike scratch cards, a guest is guaranteed to win the top prize! This game creates a great buzz at the wedding breakfast and you could even do a separate raffle with different coloured tickets for the children.

Budget busters

Here are some tips on how to give your guests favours without going broke in the process!

❀ If you really want to give out favours to your guests, but can't afford to give them to everyone, just give them to the women and children.

❀ If you're considering giving flower or vegetable seeds as favours, buy the seeds at the end of the planting season when many are on sale.

❀ If you want to give your guests a single chocolate as their favour, make your own instead of buying them. You can use the recipe in Chapter 9 to make some delicious truffles.

❀ If you are planning on having sparklers or Chinese lanterns as a finale to the day, leave these as the favours on the guests' tables.

❀ Double up the use of the favours by having them as place cards too. For example, write guests' names on biscuits or chocolates and set them on the tables.

❀ Stick to age-old tradition by giving out five sugared almonds. These will be cheaper than buying individual chocolates or other presents. You could leave a card on the tables telling your guests what the five almonds represent. For children you could swap the almonds for five jellybeans.

❀ You can easily make your own potpourri for your guests' favours and present it in small bags or homemade boxes.

❀ If you would prefer not to have individual favours, you can fill large glass vases with your favourite sweets such as jellybeans or marshmallows and place them as the centrepiece in the middle of the wedding breakfast tables. Make them look more attractive by adding layers of different colours.

❀ If you would like to have favours for your wedding abroad, buy them from the local area instead of bringing them with you. You can negotiate a good deal from a local shop and make them something really unique.

Real bride's tip

Instead of bringing favours with us all the way from England to Italy, we gave our guests a small bottle of limoncello, which was a local specialty. It worked out a lot cheaper as we got a good price from a local store and our guests really appreciated trying something Italian.'

Index